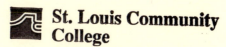

AMY TAN

Critical Companions to Popular Contemporary Writers
Kathleen Gregory Klein, Series Editor

V. C. Andrews
  by E. D. Huntley

Tom Clancy
  by Helen S. Garson

Mary Higgins Clark
  by Linda C. Pelzer

Arthur C. Clarke
  by Robin Anne Reid

James Clavell
  by Gina Macdonald

Pat Conroy
  by Landon C. Burns

Robin Cook
  by Lorena Laura Stookey

Michael Crichton
  by Elizabeth A. Trembley

Howard Fast
  by Andrew Macdonald

Ken Follett
  by Richard C. Turner

Ernest J. Gaines
  by Karen Carmean

John Grisham
  by Mary Beth Pringle

James Herriot
  by Michael J. Rossi

Tony Hillerman
  by John M. Reilly

John Irving
  by Josie P. Campbell

John Jakes
  by Mary Ellen Jones

Stephen King
  by Sharon A. Russell

Dean Koontz
  by Joan G. Kotker

Robert Ludlum
  by Gina Macdonald

Anne McCaffrey
  by Robin Roberts

Colleen McCullough
  by Mary Jean DeMarr

James A. Michener
  by Marilyn S. Severson

Anne Rice
  by Jennifer Smith

Tom Robbins
  *by Catherine E. Hoyser and
  Lorena Laura Stookey*

John Saul
  by Paul Bail

Erich Segal
  by Linda C. Pelzer

Amy Tan
  by E. D. Huntley

Leon Uris
  by Kathleen Shine Cain

Gore Vidal
  by Susan Baker and Curtis S. Gibson

AMY TAN

A Critical Companion

E. D. Huntley

CRITICAL COMPANIONS TO POPULAR CONTEMPORARY WRITERS
Kathleen Gregory Klein, Series Editor

Greenwood Press
Westport, Connecticut • London

Library of Congress Cataloging-in-Publication Data

Huntley, E. D.
    Amy Tan : a critical companion / E. D. Huntley.
      p.   cm.—(Critical companions to popular contemporary
  writers, ISSN 1082–4979)
    Includes bibliographical references and index.
    ISBN 0–313–30207–3 (alk. paper)
    1. Tan, Amy—Criticism and interpretation.   2. Women and
  literature—United States—History—20th century.   3. Chinese
  American women in literature.   4. Chinese Americans in literature.
  I. Title.   II. Series.
  PS3570.A48Z69   1998
  813'.54—dc21   97–53225

British Library Cataloguing in Publication Data is available.

Library of Congress Catalog Card Number: 97–53225
ISBN: 0–313–30207–3
ISSN: 1082–4979

First published in 1998

Greenwood Press, 88 Post Road West, Westport, CT 06881
An imprint of Greenwood Publishing Group, Inc.

Printed in the United States of America

The paper used in this book complies with the
Permanent Paper Standard issued by the National
Information Standards Organization (Z39.48–1984).

10 9 8 7 6 5 4 3 2 1

For Beowulf and Thurber, who stayed up with me and
kept me company during
many long nights when I was working on this project;
and for David, who kept them fed and walked and happy.

Contents

Series Foreword

The authors who appear in the series Critical Companions to Popular Contemporary Writers are all best-selling writers. They do not simply have one successful novel, but a string of them. Fans, critics, and specialist readers eagerly anticipate their next book. For some, high cash advances and breakthrough sales figures are automatic; movie deals often follow. Some writers become household names, recognized by almost everyone.

But, their novels are read one by one. Each reader chooses to start and, more importantly, to finish a book because of what she or he finds there. The real test of a novel is in the satisfaction its readers experience. This series acknowledges the extraordinary involvement of readers and writers in creating a best-seller.

The authors included in this series were chosen by an Advisory Board composed of high school English teachers and high school and public librarians. They ranked a list of best-selling writers according to their popularity among different groups of readers. For the first series, writers in the top-ranked group who had received no book-length, academic, literary analysis (or none in at least the past ten years) were chosen. Because of this selection method, Critical Companions to Popular Contemporary Writers meets a need that is being addressed nowhere else. The success of these volumes as reported by reviewers, librarians, and teachers led to an expansion of the series mandate to include some writers with wide critical attention—Toni Morrison, John Irving, and Maya Angelou, for example—to extend the usefulness of the series.

The volumes in the series are written by scholars with particular expertise in analyzing popular fiction. These specialists add an academic focus to the popular success that these writers already enjoy.

The series is designed to appeal to a wide range of readers. The general reading public will find explanations for the appeal of these well-known writers. Fans will find biographical and fictional questions answered. Students will find literary analysis, discussions of fictional genres, carefully organized introductions to new ways of reading the novels, and bibliographies for additional research. Whether browsing through the book for pleasure or using it for an assignment, readers will find that the most recent novels of the authors are included.

Each volume begins with a biographical chapter drawing on published information, autobiographies or memoirs, prior interviews, and, in some cases, interviews given especially for this series. A chapter on literary history and genres describes how the author's work fits into a larger literary context. The following chapters analyze the writer's most important, most popular, and most recent novels in detail. Each chapter focuses on one or more novels. This approach, suggested by the Advisory Board as the most useful to student research, allows for an in-depth analysis of the writer's fiction. Close and careful readings with numerous examples show readers exactly how the novels work. These chapters are organized around three central elements: plot development (how the story line moves forward), character development (what the reader knows of the important figures), and theme (the significant ideas of the novel). Chapters may also include sections on generic conventions (how the novel is similar or different from others in its same category of science, fantasy, thriller, etc.), narrative point of view (who tells the story and how), symbols and literary language, and historical or social context. Each chapter ends with an "alternative reading" of the novel. The volume concludes with a primary and secondary bibliography, including reviews.

The alternative readings are a unique feature of this series. By demonstrating a particular way of reading each novel, they provide a clear example of how a specific perspective can reveal important aspects of the book. In the alternative reading sections, one contemporary literary theory—way of reading, such as feminist criticism, Marxism, new historicism, deconstruction, or Jungian psychological critique—is defined in brief, easily comprehensible language. That definition is then applied to the novel to highlight specific features that might go unnoticed or be understood differently in a more general reading. Each volume defines two or three specific theories, making them part of the reader's understanding of how diverse meanings may be constructed from a single novel.

Taken collectively, the volumes in the Critical Companions to Popular Contemporary Writers series provide a wide-ranging investigation of the complexities of current best-selling fiction. By treating these novels seriously as both literary works and publishing successes, the series demonstrates the potential of popular literature in contemporary culture

Kathleen Gregory Klein
Southern Connecticut State University

Acknowledgments

Several people have helped me with this project in one way or another, but the first two who must be named and thanked are Kathleen Gregory Klein of Southern Connecticut State University and Barbara Rader of Greenwood Publishing Group who gave me the opportunity to write about one of my favorite authors. The work has been enlightening and rewarding, and I am grateful to Kathy and Barbara who made the experience possible.

My gratitude also goes to five special individuals without whom this project would have been extremely difficult for me. To Georgia Rhoades for her friendship and support—for making me take breaks and go to lunch; even when she wasn't in town, Georgia encouraged me by sending postcards. To Margaret Kilgore, who protected me from telephone calls and other interruptions during the critical rewriting stage, which coincided with a period at work that I hope never again to experience; she helped me in so many ways to stay sane in the midst of a schedule that threatened to overwhelm and engulf me. And to my three graduate assistants—Wendy Isicson, Brandi Walker, and Svetlana Babuskina—who provided invaluable help as they expertly tracked down reviews and other sources and otherwise helped me with a number of other research tasks, as well as with the index.

And finally—and always—I owe more than I can say to David Huntley who not only made my life comfortable and joyful during the project, but also took on the tasks of proofreading, formatting, and printing at the end when the demands of my job so exhausted me that this project seemed impossible to complete.

1

The Life of Amy Tan

Amy Tan was born in 1952 in Oakland, California, the only daughter of Daisy and John Tan who had both emigrated from China just a few years earlier. Amy, whose Chinese name is An-mei, meaning "Blessing from America," was the middle child. At her birth, the Tans already had a son, Peter, born in 1950; another son, named John after his father, was born in 1954. Both Daisy and John Tan had unusual backgrounds that would in due course provide their daughter with a great deal of narrative material for her novels.

During World War II, John Tan had worked for the United States Information Service, and when the war was over, he left China in 1947 for America and a new life. Although trained as an electrical engineer in Beijing, he declined a scholarship for further study at the Massachusetts Institute of Technology, deciding instead to enter the Baptist ministry.

By the time Daisy Tan came to California in 1949, she had already endured a life replete with considerable tragedy and melodrama. Born into a wealthy Shanghai family as the daughter of a scholar who had died when she was very young, Daisy spent part of her childhood in exile with her mother, Jing-mei, on an island off the coast of Shanghai. The widowed Jing-mei had been forced to become the concubine of a rich man who raped her to prevent a refusal of his proposition, and her new socially unacceptable status earned her the ostracism of her own family. Jing-mei bore the rich man a son, and when one of his principal wives took the boy away and claimed him as her own, the unhappy concubine committed suicide by swallowing a lethal quantity of raw opium infused into a New Year cake. Nine-year-old Daisy was left to grow up with neither mother nor father, and eventually, when she was of age, she entered a traditional marriage, arranged for her by relatives. The marriage produced a son who died early, and three daughters whom she was later forced to give up when she fled both the marriage and her abusive husband in 1949. Daisy ultimately managed to get a divorce, but she did not see her daughters again until 1978. Not long after the divorce, Daisy emigrated to the United States, where she met and married John Tan shortly after her arrival. Decades later, Daisy's daughter would incorporate Jing-mei's story into *The Joy Luck Club* as the tragic history of An-mei Hsu's mother.

Like thousands of Asian Americans, Amy Tan spent her childhood years attempting to understand, as well as to come to terms with and to reconcile, the contradictions between her ethnicity and the dominant Western culture in which she was being raised and educated. She lived the classic minority experience: at home, she was an uneasy American-ized teenager at odds with the expectations of her traditional Chinese parents; at school—where she frequently was the only Chinese student in her classes—she was the Asian outsider who looked different from everyone else in the predominantly white American world. Despite their earlier life-changing decisions to come to America, Daisy and John Tan continued to cling to many elements of the culture of their homeland, living an essentially insular life and socializing mainly with the members of California's Chinese community, although their ambitions for their children included a certain degree of Americanization. Like so many young second-generation Americans who have little or no experience with their parents' home countries, Amy and her brothers—to the dismay of their parents—completely embraced the American culture that dominated their experiences outside their home. Later, as an adult, Amy Tan commented on the bicultural tensions that marked her childhood and adolescence: "They [her parents] wanted us to have American circumstances and Chinese character," she told Elaine Woo of the *Los Angeles Times* (12 May 1989), using a phrase that she would attribute to Lindo Jong in *The Joy Luck Club*. Describing the kind of behavior that her parents expected, Tan went on: "We should always think like a Chinese person but we should always speak perfect English so we can take advantage of circumstances" (Woo).

Although she grew up as an almost completely assimilated Asian American, Amy Tan is well aware of the price that she and other members of minority groups have paid for their partial admission into the dominant culture:

> There was shame and self-hate. There is this myth that America is a melting pot, but what happens in assimilation is that we end up deliberately choosing the American things—hot dogs and apple pie—and ignoring the Chinese offerings. (Wang)

She points out that for so many Americans of non-European ancestry, the message from the dominant culture is that an individual from a minority group must reject the minority culture to assimilate successfully. Also implied in that message is the idea that assimilation is a necessary prerequisite to success and to achieving the American Dream.

Even today, Tan has not forgotten that when she was a child, she pinched her nose with a clothespin for a week in the hope that doing so would Westernize her Asian nose. For a time, in fact, she fantasized about plastic surgery that would transform her appearance. But the differences went far beyond facial features. She also remembers feeling "ashamed when people came over and saw my mother preparing food. She didn't make TV dinners and use canned foods. She used fresh vegetables and served fish with the heads still on. I worried people would think that we ate that because it was less expensive" (Schleier 1). Another memory reminds Tan that she worried about what her mother would bring to a school birthday party: "Would it be an exotic Chinese dish that the other kids would make fun of?" (Streitfeld F8).

Another source of disjunction for the Tan children was language. In their home, Daisy and John Tan spoke to their children in a combination that consisted of English and Mandarin, and even after Amy entered school, her mother continued to speak to her in Chinese although Amy always responded in English (Pearlman and Henderson 16). Daisy Tan never lost her Shanghai accent and never quite acquired fluent English, and her daughter still remembers classmates' taunts about her mother's Chinese-inflected speech. For her part, however, Amy seems to have resisted learning more than rudimentary conversational Chinese, and she did not study that language seriously until she became an adult. Many years later, Tan reflected on the linguistic tensions that marked her childhood and adolescence, suggesting that having parents whose English was less than fluent or idiomatic had a negative effect on her own performance in school. She points out that although she never was considered a poor student in her English classes, English was not her best subject:

> Math is precise; there is only one correct answer. Whereas, for me, at least, the answers on English tests were always a judgment call, a matter of opinion and personal experience. . . . Fortunately, I happen to be rebellious . . . and enjoy the challenge of disproving assumptions made about me. (Tan, "Mother Tongue")

Because the Tan family moved frequently while Amy and her brothers were young, Amy did much of her growing up in several California cities and towns: Oakland, Fresno, Hayward, Palo Alto, Santa Rosa, Sunnyvale, and finally Santa Clara where the family eventually settled. Tan explains the effect of that impermanency on her childhood:

> We moved almost every year or every six months. I was constantly having to make new friends, to prove myself—it made me a more introspective child, a more solitary child. . . . then I would write letters to friends, and because I thought my life was boring I would make up a life. (Jones)

And although Santa Clara would be home for a few years, the peripatetic lifestyle would resume in Tan's adolescence, ultimately taking the family far beyond California and away from the United States to Europe.

The Tans had tremendously high expectations for their children. Amy Tan remembers that from the time she was five or six, her parents articulated clear goals for her. She would become a neurosurgeon because her parents considered the brain to be the most important part of the human body, and during her spare time she would pursue a career as a concert pianist (Pearlman and Henderson 17). But parental ambitions for lucrative careers for her notwithstanding, the young Amy, who had won an essay contest when she was eight (her entry was "What the Library Means to Me"), nurtured dreams of becoming a writer. She kept her dreams to herself, however, believing that "a person doesn't make a lot of money being a writer" (Lew) and somehow instinctively understanding that her parents' ambitions for her had more to do with monetary success than with her future career satisfaction.

When Tan was fifteen, both her father and her older brother, Peter, died of malignant brain tumors within eight months of each other. John Tan's death had an unforeseen but significant effect on his family, and especially on his only daughter. Because he had been a minister, his wife—despite her emotional and psychological attachment to Chinese traditions and folkways—had worked diligently while he was alive to learn and to practice the proper (Western) Christian lifestyle. But when her husband and son both died so tragically, Daisy Tan reverted completely to the customs and belief systems of her Chinese upbringing for comfort as well as answers. She invoked the aid of Chinese deities, and she sought out the counsel of geomancers who might be able to determine whether the Tan home was contaminated with bad energies. Amy Tan, in fact, credits her mother's reaction to bereavement with introducing her to the Chinese culture that later would form the geography of her novels. Another effect of Daisy Tan's loss was her confession to her children that she had been married before she met their father, and that she had three daughters from that marriage still living in China and lost to her since that country and the United States had severed all diplomatic connections at the end of the 1940s. This startling revelation eventually found its way into Amy Tan's novels, surfacing in the history of Suyuan Woo in *The Joy Luck Club*.

Convinced that the Santa Clara house was "diseased," and disturbed by the fact that "nine bad things had happened in the neighborhood" (Lyall C6), Daisy Tan left California in 1968, taking her two remaining children on a long odyssey to New York, Washington, and Florida before they sailed across the Atlantic to the Netherlands. Driving a Volkswagen, the trio toured the Continent in search of an appropriate place to live close to an English-speaking school. They eventually settled in Montreux, Switzerland.

Daisy Tan might have believed that the move would help her family to come to terms with their tragedy, but in Switzerland, Amy rebelled against her mother and everything she stood for, joining a wild crowd and dating a German man who was rumored to associate with drug dealers. "I did a bunch of crazy things," says Amy Tan. "My mother . . . thought I should be even better as a daughter because of what had happened. . . . Instead, I just kind of went to pieces" (Marvis 77–78). But Daisy Tan had colossal reserves of strength about which her daughter knew very little. With the assistance of a private investigator, Daisy confirmed the rumors about her daughter's boyfriend and unearthed the further unsavory information that he was an escaped inmate of a

German mental hospital. Years later, Amy was able to appreciate her mother's adept handling of the situation:

> Mother engineered the biggest drug bust in the history of Montreux and got me hauled before the local magistrate. After, she drove me to the Swiss border to meet with the boyfriend. It was the smartest thing she could have done: seeing him no longer had anything to do with rebellion and I realized I wasn't interested anymore. (Ross)

The European sojourn was a milestone for Amy Tan. Uprooted from a familiar California in which her historically maligned Asian heritage clashed with the American culture that she had embraced, Amy found herself in a strange new society that had so few Asians that she was considered an attractive novelty: "Everywhere I went people stared. Europeans asked me out. I had never been asked out in America" (Wang).

In 1969, Amy Tan—all of seventeen years old—graduated from the Institut Monte Rosa Internationale, a high school in Montreux, Switzerland, and the Tan family returned to the United States, to the San Francisco area. Amy began her college career at Linfield College, a Baptist institution in Oregon chosen by her mother probably because the school was small and conservative. After two semesters, however, Amy left Linfield to transfer—much against her mother's wishes and advice—to San Jose City College because she had fallen in love and wanted to be near Louis DeMattei, her boyfriend who happened to be Italian American rather than Chinese. For Daisy Tan, however, the last straw was Amy's decision to change her major from pre-med to a double major in English and linguistics, thus ending the possibility that one of the Tan children would one day enjoy a high-paying career as a neurosurgeon. The rift between mother and daughter was significant: they did not speak to one another for six months.

Transferring once again to yet another school—San Jose State University—Amy Tan earned her baccalaureate degree in English and linguistics and her master's degree in linguistics. After graduation she married DeMattei, who was beginning a career as a tax lawyer. Because she had made no real professional plans, Amy began studying for her doctorate at the University of California campuses at Santa Cruz and at Berkeley. Before completing the degree, however, she dropped out of the doctoral program, deciding that she needed to do something other than continuing to be a student (Pearlman and Henderson 17). Once again, Daisy

Tan's ambition of having a daughter who had "Dr." in front of her name was thwarted.

During her college years and afterward, Amy had worked her way through some widely differing jobs—switchboard operator, carhop for an A&W franchise, bartender and pizza maker at The Round Table—and when she made the decision not to continue as a doctoral student, she again tried her hand at a variety of careers. She started as a Language Development consultant to the Alameda County Association for Retarded Citizens, and she later directed training programs for developmentally disabled children. In the latter position, the ethnic issues that she had faced as she was growing up resurfaced and gave her cause for concern. As one of the small number of Asian Americans working in language development, and as the sole minority project director for the Bureau of Handicapped Children, Tan soon found herself serving uncomfortably as the representative minority member on various councils and task forces:

> What bothered me was . . . that they would think that one Chinese American could represent American Indians, and blacks, and hispanics. Chinese Americans are very different from immigrants . . . from Thailand and Cambodia and Vietnam. (Pearlman and Henderson 17)

Uncomfortable with the role that she increasingly was being asked to play, Amy Tan left her administrative job and once again changed careers, and this time she became a full-time writer.

At first joining a friend who ran a medical publishing company, Tan eventually moved into freelance business writing. So successful was she in this new venture that she was able to purchase a house for her mother, who finally began to believe that perhaps her daughter was successful after all. Tan explains, "That's really what success is about in Chinese families—it's not success for yourself, it's success so you can take care of your family" (Somogyi and Stanton).

As a freelance writer, Amy Tan produced a wide array of projects for several major corporations: training manuals for AT&T sales personnel who were assigned to promote "Reach Out America," business proposals for national consulting firms, and even a book for IBM, *Telecommunications and You*, aimed at systems engineers and company CEOs who were involved with the growing telecommunications field. She also worked on projects for Bank of America and Pacific Bell. Tan admits that she had wonderful clients who allowed her a great deal of latitude in her choice of projects. In addition, she was well paid, and the day finally came when she was able to say to her mother, "I can do well enough to take care of you for the rest of your life" (Somogyi and Stanton 27).

Success brought Amy Tan a new set of problems. The demand for her services as a writer was so high that she was accepting too many projects. In a two-month marathon of work, she clocked ninety billable hours a week; but at the same time, she came to the conclusion that her work, though lucrative, failed to satisfy her. She felt trapped, and remembers telling herself every morning how much she hated her work (Pearlman and Henderson 18). Determined to put her life to rights, she went into therapy to learn to manage her workaholic tendencies. That strategy ended abruptly when she discontinued the sessions after her psychiatrist fell asleep three times while she was talking to him:

> I would talk about feeling good, and he'd fall asleep. But if I recalled something from my childhood that was traumatic, and I was crying, he was very attentive. And I thought, he's reinforcing me to be unhappy. (Streitfeld)

At that point, she embarked on her own plan to get her life in order: She took up jazz piano and began attempting to write only what she wanted to (Pearlman and Henderson 18). She also read extensively— fiction by Alice Munro, Eudora Welty, Flannery O'Connor, Amy Hempel, and Mary Robeson, as well as John Gardner's *The Art of Fiction*. She especially liked Louise Erdrich's work, which held particular resonance for Tan who was "amazed by her [Erdrich's] voice. It was different and yet it seemed I could identify with the powerful images, the beautiful language and such moving stories" (Feldman 24). Erdrich's novel *Love Medicine* was for Tan a particularly powerful influence with its collection of narratives shared by storytellers from several generations of a Native American family. Indeed, influenced by the work of Erdrich and others, Tan has successfully employed as a narrative strategy the juxtaposition of multiple points of view with their origins in different times and geographies.

During her period of self-designed therapy, Tan wrote her first short story, a piece about a Chinese chess prodigy who has a difficult relationship with her strong-willed and overbearing mother. That story, "Endgame," was Tan's ticket to the Squaw Valley Community of Writers, a workshop directed by novelist Oakley Hall who also taught at the

University of California in Irvine. At the workshop, described by Tan as "intensely emotional, exhilarating," Tan met writers Amy Hempel and Molly Giles. After they had a chance to read Tan's work, Hempel advised Tan to "look for the news in my story, and to go for the things that are the most uncomfortable" (Feldman 24). Giles, who had recently won the Flannery O'Connor award, told her, "You don't have a story here; you have a dozen," and then helped her to revise "Endgame" (Pearlman and Henderson 19). The story was published in *FM Magazine* and later reprinted in *Seventeen*. Heartened by her initial success, Tan sent her second attempt, "Waiting Between the Trees," to the *New Yorker*, which rejected it. Meanwhile, the fledgling writer joined a new writers' group formed by Molly Giles in San Francisco.

Thanks to Giles, a copy of "Endgame" came to the attention of a California-based literary agent named Sandra Dijkstra who was impressed enough to encourage Tan to continue writing. A chance occurrence triggered the next step in Amy Tan's nascent writing career. When a friend telephoned to congratulate Tan for achieving the status of an internationally known writer, Tan discovered with horror that "Endgame" had been translated and published in Italy without either her knowledge or her permission. Remembering Sandra Dijkstra's encouragement, Tan asked Dijkstra to represent her. The agent asked to see more of Tan's work before making a decision, and Tan responded with a copy of "Waiting Between the Trees" accompanied by a letter in which she explained that she had written the story "as an experiment to see if it would develop into a novel or series of related short stories about different generations and perspectives of women in balance or out of balance with themselves and each other" (Feldman 24–25). On the basis of two stories and an idea, Dijkstra agreed to become Amy Tan's agent. The partnership would prove to be significant, not just for writer and agent but also for American fiction.

In 1986, Amy Tan received a profound shock. Her mother was hospitalized for what seemed to be a heart attack, and although the problem turned out to be angina, Amy was shaken enough to examine seriously her relationship with her mother who had often complained that her daughter knew very little about her (Pearlman and Henderson 19). Realizing the truth of her mother's comment, Tan vowed at that point to listen when her mother told stories, and to accompany Daisy Tan to China if necessary. That vow would turn out to be an important moment in Tan's development as a writer.

When Tan sent a third short story to Sandra Dijkstra, the agent asked for outlines and synopses for additional narratives. Tan recalls her puzzled surprise when Dijkstra said, "I think we're ready to sell a book" (18). Nevertheless, she complied with the request, and in July 1987 produced a proposal for a collection of short stories that she called *Wind and Water*. In October of that year, Amy and her husband traveled with Daisy Tan to China. It was Amy's first trip to the homeland of her parents, and while in China, she finally met her half-sisters—Daisy's three daughters from her first unhappy marriage. She also found, to her surprise, that China was not alien to her. As she points out, "I felt that in some way I belonged, that I had found a country related to me" (21). The journey gave Tan a deeper understanding of the two cultures in her heritage, the inevitable tensions that exist between those cultures, and the richness of her own experiences and those of her mother as they both negotiated their way between cultures. Significantly, it was during that China journey that Amy Tan's new career was born—back in the United States.

The story of *The Joy Luck Club* is the stuff of publishing legend. When Amy Tan returned home from China, she was astounded by the news that Dijkstra had negotiated for her a $50,000 contract for a book that would be published by G. P. Putnam's Sons. Before the China trip, Dijkstra had persuaded Tan to rename the collection, using the title of one of the stories; and it was as *The Joy Luck Club* that the book was scheduled for publication. Inspired by the bidding war that had culminated in the lucrative contract for her as-yet-unwritten book, Amy Tan quit her freelance writing business and finished that first full-length manuscript in four months, delivering it to the publisher in pristine condition, described by Tan's editor, Faith Sale, as "clean as anything you've ever seen, in perfect white boxes, imprinted with the 'Joy Luck' chop Amy's mother had encouraged her to have made while in China and tied with red ribbon" (Feldman 25).

The Joy Luck Club was a critical and popular success, selling over four million copies and earning nominations for or winning a number of prestigious literary awards. With a release date of March 1989, the novel appeared on the *New York Times* bestseller list the next month, rising to fourth place on that list. In 1993, a stage adaptation created by American playwright Susan Kim, and produced through a major collaborative effort between the Yale-China Association, the Shanghai People's Art Theatre, and Connecticut's Long Wharf Theatre, was performed with a predominantly Chinese cast in several Chinese cities including Shanghai and Beijing. The following year, a film based on the novel, with a screenplay by Amy Tan, was released in the United States.

Despite her success, Tan was once again forced to deal with her mother's high expectations for her. "Hmm. No. 4. Who is this No. 3? No. 2? No. 1?" asked Daisy Tan, as always the mother who was ambitious for her daughter. And then, as though realizing what she was saying, she immediately added, "I'm not disappointed you're No. 4; I just think you're so good that you always deserve to be No. 1" (Marvis 83). But Daisy Tan's pride in her daughter's accomplishments was palpably obvious outside the family circle. "She's busy going to bookstores to see if they have the book," Amy revealed after the publication of *The Joy Luck Club*. "If they don't, she scolds them" (83).

With the novel on bestseller lists, Daisy Tan revised her expectations for her daughter. Amy Tan reveals that her mother began saying, "I always knew you'd be a writer" (Somogyi and Stanton 27), crediting Amy's wild imagination as the inspiration for that prophecy. Tan's own recollections are quite different. In her memory, her mother blamed that same wild imagination for Amy's propensity for getting into trouble.

In the wake of Tan's first success came a second novel, *The Kitchen God's Wife*, published in 1991, and inspired to a large extent by Daisy Tan's life in China. That second book also attracted a great deal of positive popular and critical attention, and the possibility of a film version has been discussed seriously. Two children's books followed: *The Moon Lady* (1992) and *The Chinese Siamese Cat* (1994). In 1996, Tan's third novel, *The Hundred Secret Senses*, was published, and like the two previous novels, it combines autobiographical elements with episodes and images from Daisy Tan's stories. In addition to her novels, Amy Tan has published a number of short stories for both children and adults, in a variety of journals and periodicals. Her oeuvre is not limited to fiction. Two highly regarded essays on language—"The Language of Discretion" (1990) and "Mother Tongue" (1991)—focus on the connections between ethnic identity and language, providing for readers a cultural and theoretical background for Tan's fiction as well as for the works of other writers of non-Western ancestry. Tan also has written essays for several popular periodicals including *Life*, *Glamour*, and *Ladies Home Journal*.

CRITICAL RECEPTION

Thanks to the success of *The Joy Luck Club*, Amy Tan may well be one of the best-known American writers of Asian ancestry. Remaining on the *New York Times* bestseller list for nearly a year after publication, *The Joy Luck Club* was short-listed for the National Book Award for Fiction and nominated for the National Book Critics Circle Award. In recognition of her achievement, Tan received the Bay Area Book Reviewers Award for fiction as well as the Commonwealth Club Gold Award. In addition to her $50,000 contract, Amy Tan received around $1.2 million from Vintage for the paperback rights for *The Joy Luck Club*. The novel has been translated into at least twenty languages, including Chinese.

Critical commentary on *The Joy Luck Club* was highly complimentary. "The only negative thing I could ever say about this book is that I'll never again be able to read it for the first time," wrote novelist Carolyn See (*Current Biography Yearbook* 562). In his review for the *New York Times Book Review*, Orville Schell writes that Amy Tan has "a wonderful eye for what is telling, a fine ear for dialogue, a deep empathy for her subject matter, and a guilelessly straightforward way of writing" (3). Even those critics who were not overwhelmingly positive about the novel found praiseworthy elements in Tan's prose. Writing that *The Joy Luck Club* "is lively but not terribly deep," Rhoda Koenig goes on to say, "One cannot help being charmed, however, by the sharpness of observation, the mixture of familiarity and strangeness, and finally the universality of Tan's themes" (82). In *New Statesman & Society*, British critic Carole Angier points out the flaws in the novel, but concedes that "*The Joy Luck Club* is *very* cunningly crafted," and that "all of it is interesting: Chinese customs, ideas and superstitions; the contrast between Chinese suffering and strength, American ease and unhappiness" (35).

Like its predecessor, *The Kitchen God's Wife* garnered substantial critical approbation, in some cases, from writers who found it more appealing than they did *The Joy Luck Club*. Rhoda Koenig of *New York* magazine described *Kitchen God* as "a novel even better than the bouncy, touching stories of *The Joy Luck Club*" (83). Commentary on Tan's new novel was superlative. Sybil Steinberg called it "a triumph, a solid indication of a mature talent for magically involving storytelling, beguiling use of language and deeply textured and nuanced character development" (45); Gil Schwartz observed, "Few contemporary books feel like literature. This one does" (116); and Ann Fisher, writing for the *Library Journal*, pointed out that "The rhythms of Winnie's [the central character] story are spellbinding and true, without the contrivance common in many modern novels" (198).

So well received were Amy Tan's first two novels that when *The Hundred Secret Senses* was published, readers and critics expected another book like the first two. Instead, they were treated to a new portrait of Tan's fictional landscape, one that includes collisions between present and past, the actual and the imaginary, this life and the afterlife, skepticism and mysticism—with a whimsical overlay of the supernatural. Critical opinion of *The Hundred Secret Senses* was mixed, ranging from Laura Shapiro's assertion that it is "more finely nuanced than her [Tan's] previous two" (92) to Claire Messud's description of the novel as "a mildly entertaining and slightly ridiculous ghost story" (11). Some reviewers commented that the novel's ending was less than satisfactory, that events were too neatly wrapped up, and that they had difficulty in accepting the denouement involving Olivia's near-spiritual conversion. Nevertheless, the preponderance of critical commentary was, on the whole, positive with a few reservations. Writing for the *Library Journal*, Sheila Riley describes the novel as "haunting," and calls it "a mysterious believable story" (101) and Laura Shapiro suggests that Amy Tan "doesn't simply return to a world but burrows more deeply into it, following new trails to fresh revelations" (92). Several other writers point out that Kwan, whose voice dominates the novel, is probably Tan's most original and memorable character creation. An unsigned review in *Publishers' Weekly* mentions "the pleasure of Tan's seductive prose and the skill with which she unfolds the many-layered narrative" (74), and Diane Fortuna notes that "what most commends the novel are the fragments of actual Chinese history, so exotically retrieved that the reader hurries through the modern narrative in order to learn more about the past" (28).

AMY TAN AS A WRITER

Her childhood dreams notwithstanding, Amy Tan did not originally set out to be a novelist. Highly successful and fairly comfortably settled with her growing career as a freelance business writer, and working with clients whom she liked, she nevertheless dabbled in fiction writing as a hobby, as something enjoyable and not strictly work-related. Her decision to slow down and begin engaging in activities that fulfilled her creative side facilitated her transformation from workaholic business writer to fiction writer, and the membership in Molly Giles's writers' group propelled Tan well on her way toward completing the transition. With the publication of *The Joy Luck Club*, she became Amy Tan, the novelist and fiction writer.

It is clear that Tan enjoys writing so much that it has become her life. She remembers that writing her first novel was a magical experience:

> I'd light incense, put on certain music, and start to imagine
> myself in another world. I conjured up people to come and
> tell me their stories. Then I'd enter that other world and hours
> would go by and I'd forget everything else. (Feldman 25)

That "other world" is Tan's fictional universe, a world that exists primarily in her imagination—a place that allows her to visualize the characters whose stories she is writing. For Tan, the ability and the time to
enter that dream world are crucial to her creative process:

> I focus on a specific image, and that image takes me into a
> scene. Then I begin to see the scene and I ask myself, "What's
> to your right? What's to your left?" and I open up into this
> fictional world. I often play music as a way of blocking out
> the rest of my consciousness, so I can enter into this world
> and let it go where it wants to go, wherever the characters
> want to go. (Epel 284)

Not surprisingly, dreams appear frequently in Tan's novels, and they
function as a dominant motif in *The Hundred Secret Senses*.

One of the constants in Amy Tan's writing career is her wide circle of
friends who are also writers. Still an active member of the writing group
that Molly Giles founded after the Squaw Valley workshop, Tan says
that she could not have written *The Joy Luck Club* without the group's
support, and she adds that Giles is "the only writing teacher I've ever
had." Although she travels constantly to speaking engagements or on
promotional tours for her books, Tan maintains her connection with the
writing group, a core of five or six writers who meet once a week, frequently at Tan's home in San Francisco's Presidio Heights. She credits
those meetings with keeping her on a writing schedule and honing her
own editorial skills. During the meetings, group members meet and read
their work aloud to the others, who respond with suggestions for the
writer, with what Tan describes as "a real reader's response" (Pearlman
and Henderson 19).

Working with a group that she can trust to provide honest evaluations
aids Tan in the extensive revision process through which she goes while
she is working on a book. She has commented in many interviews that
she revises each page of her work anywhere from twelve to twenty times,
reading her text aloud so that she can hear the rhythm of her prose. By

her estimate, she went through several thousand sheets of paper while she was writing *The Joy Luck Club*.

AMY TAN AS STORYTELLER

In her novels, Amy Tan allows her characters to employ storytelling as a device for shaping their histories and making coherent sense of the significant events of their lives. For these characters, storytelling is a means of keeping the past alive and building a bridge between it and the present, of transmitting cultural codes and rituals, of subtly educating their daughters, and finally of somehow imprinting the essence of their selves on the next generation.

Tan is especially gifted at weaving multiple stories with a variety of narrators into the intricate fabric of each book. Tan herself has recognized her own ability to construct distinctive and memorable narratives, commenting that her storytelling gifts are responsible in large measure for the ongoing popularity—with readers and critics alike—of her work. She has said that her childhood exposure to Bible stories as well as "tons of fairy tales, both Grimm and Chinese" (Wang) has made stories a significant element in her writing, and she credits her parents with both instilling in her the impulse to tell stories and providing her with models for unforgettable tales. In an interview with Gretchen Giles, Amy Tan reveals that she learned the craft of story construction from her father, a very busy Baptist minister who managed to spend quality time with his children by reading his sermons to them and then asking for their opinions on content and language. Tan recalls that her father's sermons were written in narrative form, as carefully crafted stories. She also points out that in contrast to her father's carefully designed narratives, most of her mother's stories were neither formally constructed nor refined, but rather evolved out of the daily life, activities, and conversations of the extended Tan family. Daisy Tan, a talented natural storyteller, exchanged family news and stories of local events with other women—close friends and extended family—as they sat preparing vegetables or other ingredients for cooking. Tan remembers her mother and aunts "gossiping about the family, and going on for hours and hours about some little detail that they found disgusting in some relative or friend" (Giles). Tan describes her mother as "a wonderful storyteller, for observation of character, emotional truth and passion," although she adds, "She needs a lot of editing because her stories are all over the place" (Lyall C6). Daisy Tan's tales might have seemed to be "all over the place," but they had one important element—the powerful and haunting images that ultimately became Amy Tan's novels.

A veritable anthology of stories—both tragic and comic—emerged from Daisy Tan's treasure chest of memories after her bout with angina. Amy Tan recalls that when she heard the news that her mother had been taken to the hospital, she was reminded that very recently her mother had said, "If I die, what would you remember?" (Feldman 25). Stung by remorse, Amy realized that she had never truly listened to her mother's tales of life in China, that she had only a sketchy outline of her mother's history, and she promised herself that she would get to know her mother in the time that they had left together, that she would discover what Daisy Tan's life had been like before she emigrated to America for a chance at a fresh start. Amy Tan found in her mother's life a wealth of material for her writing. There were stories about Daisy's mother committing suicide by swallowing pure opium with her New Year rice cakes, about the difficulties of World War II in China, about arranged marriages between women and men who barely knew each other, about Daisy's first husband to whom she always referred as "that bad man." One story that seems to have intrigued Tan was her mother's account of a friend who was fleeing from the approaching Japanese troops. The friend was carrying all of her belongings in bags that she finally began dropping one by one as her strength gave out and the bags grew more difficult to carry. That vignette surfaced in *The Joy Luck Club*, translated into the poignant story of how Suyuan Woo, during her flight from the Japanese, had to drop bag after bag of food and clothes for her twin babies until finally, in utter exhaustion, she left those babies beside the road in the hope that kind strangers would take them home and give them the care that Suyuan no longer could provide. Daisy's tales—which eventually found their way into her daughter's novels, especially into *The Kitchen God's Wife*—were a revelation to Amy who had no inkling that her mother had lived such a dramatic and turbulent—and exotically alien—life before she married John Tan. As she listened to her mother, Amy began to understand Daisy's tremendous need to tell her stories:

> She wanted someone to go back and relive [sic] her life with her. It was a way for her to exorcise her demons, and for me to finally listen and empathize and learn what memory means, and what you can change about the past. (Lyall C6)

Piecing together the fragments of her mother's remembered life, Amy Tan has created a body of work that explores the nature of memory—what it is, how it functions, what it means, how it shapes an individual. In *The Hundred Secret Senses*, memory becomes the vehicle by which the past reconfigures the present, and through which the present revises the past.

In an interview with Julie Lew, Tan explained that she wrote her first stories in an attempt to explain herself and her thoughts to her mother.

> I wanted her [Daisy Tan] to know what I thought about China and . . . growing up in this country. And I wanted those words to almost fall off the page so that she could just see the story. (23)

Gradually, Amy began to realize that she did remember fragments of stories from her childhood, bits and pieces of her mother's reminiscences, images and episodes from tales about life in China. As a matter of fact, she was surprised to discover that she did have a considerable—if imagistic and impressionistic—knowledge about Chinese culture, and she has been particularly pleased to find out that her work resonates as strongly with Chinese readers as it does with the general reading public.

Tan views storytelling as a particularly appropriate narrative strategy for her fiction through which she seeks to tease out some form of truth from many points of view. She notes, as well, that storytelling enables her to reflect on the issues with which she and her mother have grappled in their own lives—concerns that are familiar in various ways to Tan's readers, many of whom have struggled with the same concerns in different settings. Tan points out that as someone who was raised on the border between cultures, she was confronted with values and ideas that appeared contradictory, and those contradictions raised many questions in her mind. For Tan, those questions have provided "a filter for looking at all my experiences and seeing them from different angles." She goes on to suggest that storytellers ask those same kinds of questions, that "underneath the surface of the story is a question or a perspective or a nagging little emotion" (Giles). The women at the center of Tan's novels give shape to their lives through stories that afford them a way to codify and organize their experiences, and more importantly, to transmit those experiences to others (daughters, sisters) whose lives have been profoundly affected—whether consciously or unconsciously—by aggregated impact of those experiences.

By crafting her novels as records of the act of storytelling, Tan is working in an honored and ancient Chinese tradition called *talk story* (*gong gu tsai*), a felicitous combination of genres from Chinese oral tradition articulated in local vernaculars in narrative form. (For a fuller discussion of talk story, see Chapter 2.) The tradition provides Tan with the ideal medium for bringing to life the inhabitants of a fictional universe that encompasses two centuries, two cultures, two nations, and multiple generations—separated by space, time, and language. Moreover, through talk story, Tan is able to combine seemingly random fragments of stories from a variety of speakers who have different perspectives into a coherent and meaningful whole, thus providing readers of each novel with a continuous, albeit nonlinear, narrative that engages, challenges, and ultimately provokes reflection.

2

Amy Tan and Asian American Literature

Like a growing number of contemporary writers, Amy Tan crafts novels that resist facile and definitive classification into any of the conventional fictional genres. That the books are novels is widely acknowledged, although Tan has said that she intended *The Joy Luck Club* to be a collection of short stories. Readers and critics alike do, however, agree that Tan's work incorporates or echoes other genres including nonfiction and poetry. In fact, a significant source of the charm and artistry of the three Tan novels is their shape as fictional narratives that embrace elements of biography and autobiography, history and mythology, folk tale and Asian talk story, personal reminiscence and memoir. Tan's novels reify and reinterpret traditional genres by casting them in a variety of modes—realistic, comic, tragic, tragicomic, allegorical, fantastic, naturalistic, and heroic—that metamorphose seamlessly into each other in Tan's signature narrative style. Commentary is juxtaposed with memory, fable with history, pidgin English with California-speak, American culture with Chinese tradition, past with present in a collision of stories and voices and personalities, filtered through the point of view of an Asian American author who lives between worlds, who inhabits that border country known only to those in whose minds and sensibilities cultures clash and battle for dominance. Although Amy Tan's prose style is distinctively her own, she also owes a literary debt to other writers who, like her, inhabit the border country that shapes and inspires so many

minority writers—writers who derive their voices and narrative structures from their experiences in the neighborhoods of America's diaspora
cultures.

ASIAN AMERICAN LITERATURE: A DEFINITION

In 1982, Elaine Kim's ground-breaking study, *Asian American Literature:
An Introduction to the Writings and Social Context*, essentially brought an
entire body of little known literature into the American literary consciousness, and helped Asian American literature gain recognition as a
significant body of writing with both a "new tradition" of literary creation and a discernible—and very fluid—canon. In her work, Kim defined Asian American literature as "published creative writings in
English by Americans of Chinese, Japanese, Korean, and Filipino descent" (xi). Although that definition lost its currency as immigrants from
Cambodia, Vietnam, India, Pakistan, and other Asian countries began to
make their homes in the United States and to write about their experiences, one crucial element of Kim's definition still holds true. Asian
American literature is the creative work of writers of Asian descent who
identify themselves as Americans and who view their own experiences
and the world through the dual lenses of their American identities and
their ethnic roots. More specifically, Asian American literature "eluci-
dates the social history of Asians in the United States" (xiii). Although,
as Kim points out, Asian American literature "shares with most other
literature thematic concerns such as love, desire for personal freedom
and acceptance, and struggles against oppression and injustice" (xii–xiii),
this body of literature also is the product of other distinctive cultural
forces. Like African American writing, fiction, poetry, and drama by
Asian Americans is shaped by racism—both overt and disguised—and
its corollaries, prejudice and discrimination. Moreover, for most Asian
American writers, the Old Country and its culture are neither ancient
nor buried history but very much alive and integral to the present, either
in their own lives or in those of their parents and grandparents. The
immigrant experience looms large in the writing of Asian Americans,
and with that experience comes questions about marginality and life on
the border, as well as explorations of issues of biculturalism and language, and decisions about identity.

THE ASIAN AMERICAN LITERARY TRADITION

The history of Asian Americans goes back to the nineteenth century when thousands of men left their families and homes in China, Japan, Korea, and the Philippines to seek their fortunes in the United States, a country that the Chinese referred to as *gum san* or "the Gold Mountain." Seeking opportunity and possibly wealth, these men found ready work on the railroad, in gold- and silver-mining towns, and in lumber camps in the Western United States, industriously setting about making lives for themselves and for the picture brides from China and Japan who eventually traveled to the United States to marry men they had never met. The earliest official immigrant arrivals seem to have been men from Guangdong Province in China, although there exist records of Chinese sailors who stopped briefly in Baltimore in the late eighteenth century. Perhaps because they were first to arrive, the Chinese formed the largest Asian immigrant group, and they became the first Asians to experience institutionalized discrimination when the Chinese Exclusion Act of 1882 was passed by Congress, barring the majority of Chinese from entering the United States. The only exceptions to the ban were businessmen, diplomats, teachers, and students. When the law expired, it was renewed for another decade. Similar laws passed in 1902 and 1904, made the Chinese exclusion permanent, and Chinese who were already in the United States not only were denied citizenship but also were abused, publicly denounced in the press and from the pulpit, vilified, and physically attacked and even killed. Not until 1943 was exclusion legally ended with the passage of the Magnuson Act, which allowed 105 Chinese immigrants to enter the United States legally each year and gave Chinese the privilege of earning citizenship through naturalization. The older generation that is portrayed in Amy Tan's novels represents that group of new Chinese immigrants—especially the women who had long been denied entry—who entered the United States after the war in the years immediately following the Magnuson Act.

Not surprisingly, Asian immigrants—whose straight black hair and yellow-brown skin made them look different and who spoke languages that had no relation to Indo-European—seemed exotic and thus oddly fascinating to most Americans who were of European ancestry. Consequently, a number of stereotypical Asian characters became fixtures in certain forms of popular entertainment and literature. Racist images—

the result of fear, ignorance, and xenophobia—were dominant, disseminated, and encouraged in a culture that feared that the increasing numbers of Chinese laborers, who were willing to work long hours at difficult tasks for low wages, posed a threat to employment opportunities for white men. Many of these fictional Asians were "inscrutable," humorlessly industrious, humble, patient, and inclined to say "Ah so" in response to nearly any comment or question that they presumably did not understand. The few who differed were aristocratic mandarins whose haughty demeanor and elegant carriage hinted at long acquaintance with a more ceremonious way of life in a mythical Old China. For decades, Charlie Chan, Fu Manchu, and Anna May Wong were the only Asians that many Americans had ever encountered, and their images remained indelibly etched into the American imagination and popular culture until well into the twentieth century.

Despite the popularity of Asian stock characters on stage and screen and in fiction, literary work by authors of Asian ancestry, while not unknown, was not particularly accessible or available, and much of what was published rapidly went out of print. Before their arrival in the United States, most Asian immigrants had belonged to economic or social classes that, in their home countries, would have provided them with little or no exposure to education, and certainly not to art and poetry, although a few might have learned some rudimentary reading and writing. On their arrival in America, they found employment that required them to labor up to twenty hours each day, often seven days a week, focusing all of their energies on the struggle to earn livelihoods for themselves as well as for their families who remained in China or Japan or Korea. Ignored on the job, and left to socialize among themselves, few Asian immigrants learned much English beyond the few phrases that were essential to basic communication in their jobs. Overworked, underpaid, housed in barely habitable structures in labor camps, deprived of educational opportunities, and widely discriminated against, most Asian immigrants endured bleak and joyless existences that stifled all creative or imaginative impulses. Hence, the dearth of imaginative writing from the earliest Asian Americans. Early immigrant writing—when it existed at all—generally took the form of letters and journals in languages other than English. Creative efforts, which were rare, resulted mainly in unfamiliar poetic genres such as *haiku* or *tanka*. In a poignantly significant series of attempts at artistic expression, anonymous Chinese immigrants who were detained at the Angel Island Detention Center after the passage of the Exclusion Act scrawled poetry on the walls, giving vent to their emotions and disappointments (Lim and Ling 5).

Although the Exclusion Act was directed at Chinese immigrants, negative Asian stereotypes were applied indiscriminately for decades not only to Chinese but also to Japanese, Korean, and Filipino immigrants. World War II changed those perceptions when international hostilities and American military losses in the Pacific unleashed waves of anti-Japanese propaganda, accompanied by sympathy for China and the Philippines. Because China was suffering the ravages of America's enemy, the Japanese army, the Chinese in America found themselves suddenly accepted as members of a "model minority" that was praised for loyalty to the United States.

In spite of the obstacles that barred the way to an Asian literary tradition in the United States, a few pieces of writing—chiefly memoirs—by Asians did appear as early as the end of the nineteenth century. The authors—mainly Chinese—had come to the United States as students, diplomats, or merchants, and were thus exempt from the Exclusion Act. Among the early books was a series of volumes by Western-educated young men of different countries, including two from China and Korea. These books, which were commissioned by the D. Lothrop Publishing Company, focused on elucidating for the benefit of the average American reader the cultural mores and traditional customs of the writers' native countries. Other autobiographies, written in the 1930s and 1940s, attempted to perform much the same anthropological function—to describe and explain to Western readers the more attractive elements of life in China: dress, food, festivals, sports, rituals and ceremonies, leisure activities, and daily life. Common to all of these personal accounts of life in China was their limited focus on the experiences of a privileged class, the members of which had nothing in common with the hordes of Asian laborers who spent their days patiently enduring their work in America's railroads, mines, and lumber camps. These early autobiographies and memoirs entranced American readers with descriptions of Chinese houses furnished with silk carpets and decorated with jade and porcelain artifacts, surrounded by gardens burgeoning with exotic blooms, meticulously maintained by happy, smiling servants who existed to make life easy and pleasant for the family who owned the house and land.

Among the most widely read of the Asian memoir-writers between the wars were three immigrant Chinese authors whose work is representative of the style of immigrant writing that American readers—and critics and reviewers—found not only acceptable but also immensely fascinating. The most prolific of these writers was Lin Yutang, who churned out scores of essays that are most notable for their gentle self-deprecating humor—at the expense not only of the author but also of his fellow Chinese—and for their genially superficial treatment of cultural issues and questions.

In a writing career that spanned about forty years, Lin Yutang claimed that his main purpose was to explain China and her people to Western readers. That he succeeded in reaching his target audience is evident in the popularity of his works, especially *My Country and My People* (1935), a book that went through four editions. The appeal of Lin's book for the majority of readers from the 1930s through the 1960s lies in its validation of a popular myth—the stereotype of the gently bred Chinese as naive, unworldly people who desired nothing more than to focus their energies and time on artistic and literary activities, and who submitted docilely to colonial rule because they lacked the motivation to govern themselves. Not surprisingly, more than a few Asian American readers took exception to Lin Yutang's portraits of China and the Chinese, claiming that Lin's books privileged a tiny percentage of the Chinese population—the affluent classes—and ignored the reality of the impoverished majority from whose ranks most Chinese immigrants came.

With a literary output that was far less voluminous than Lin Yutang's, Pardee Lowe and Jade Snow Wong nevertheless published highly regarded and extremely well-received memoirs of their experiences as Chinese immigrants growing up in America. Like Lin Yutang's books, Pardee Lowe's *Father and Glorious Descendant* (1943) and Jade Snow Wong's *Fifth Chinese Daughter* (1945 and 1950) describe an ethnic world in which existing stereotypes are confirmed and sanitized. Both books provided the predominantly white readership of the war years with a picture of Chinese American life that was both intriguing and easy to accept as genuine because it conformed to the mythical China that already existed in the popular American consciousness. Because he had enlisted in the U.S. Army, Lowe was praised for his patriotism and for the message of accommodation and assimilation that he disseminated through his memoirs.

As valuable as these works are in the history of Asian writing in the United States, they focus mainly on those immigrants whose antecedents had belonged to the privileged classes, and the prose and images appear dated to the late twentieth-century reader. The world of Lowe and Wong is populated with tea-sipping, poetry-writing aristocrats in beautiful, alien settings that exist only in a world that has receded into memory or survives only in the pages of forgotten volumes on neglected library shelves.

After the successes of Lowe and Wong, little by Asian American writers appeared for over two decades. In 1963, however, Virginia Lee's *The House that Tai Ming Built* revived the semi-autobiographical strain of immigrant writing popularized by Lowe and Wang. Like her predecessors, Lee portrayed a Chinese culture that did not represent the experience of the majority of Chinese Americans; nevertheless, like those earlier writers, Lee is important in the history of Asian American literary production. In their introduction to the first anthology of Asian American writing, Kai-yu Hsu and Helen Palubinskas comment on the work of Lowe, Wong, and Lee, which they describe as autobiographical and suggestive of

> the Chinese culture described in the connoisseurs' manuals of Chinese jade or oolong tea, and the stereotype of the Chinese immigrant, either withdrawn and totally Chinese, or quietly assimilated and unobtrusively American. (10)

Hsu and Palubinskas also caution against dismissing those early memoirs as irrelevant, pointing out that they have value for the student of Asian American literature. They assert that the three volumes of memoirs have a genuine claim to be considered landmarks in the development of a literary tradition by Asian Americans because "the authors wrote about the Chinese in America as they saw and understood them." Hsu and Palubinskas go on to issue a challenge: "Other Chinese-American writers, if they have different perceptions, should come forth with their stories" (10). Less than a decade after the publication of Lee's book, a vocal group of those "other . . . writers" emerged onto the American literary scene. But before they did so, their work was anticipated by Louis Chu whose 1961 novel, *Eat a Bowl of Tea*, first articulated some of the major concerns that would inform the work of later Asian writers.

Eat a Bowl of Tea is remarkable for its early treatment of the debilitating effects of racism and the patriarchal culture in Asian American communities. Set in 1947, two years after the War Bride Act of 1945 opened U.S. immigration to Chinese women, the novel examines the conflict between old-world patriarchal immigrant elders and their American-born children, a struggle that Ruth Hsiao describes as involving "emotionally damaged sons and daughters locked in battles of independence with their fathers or with the tradition that gives the fathers power" (54). Louis Chu foregrounds a nascent antipatriarchal movement through a complicated plot that portrays the traditional authoritarian father as a mere parody of the traditional patriarch. Hsiao points out that many consider Chu to be "a herald of the new Asian American sensibility" (153), although she criticizes his novel for suggesting in the end that patriarchy is an incurable condition in bicultural Asian communities and for positing "the birth of a new age patriarchy" (152). Nonetheless, it is clear that Chu does indeed prefigure not only the work of the writer-activists who would follow him in the next decade, but also the even more significant explosion of writing by Asian women that would mark the 1980s and 1990s.

The new Asian American writers of the 1970s were neither completely Asian nor definitively Western, but considered themselves to be members of a distinct new culture or set of cultures. Frank Chin, one of the new writers, articulated his position vis-à-vis the dominant landscape into which he was expected to assimilate by explaining the cultural force behind his writing:

> The sensibility, the kind of sensibility that is neither Chinese of China nor white-American. The sensibility derived from the peculiar experience of a Chinese born in this country some thirty years ago, with all the stigmas attached to his race, but felt by himself alone as an individual human being. (quoted in Hsu and Palubinskas 47)

The "sensibility" of which Chin speaks was shared by his peers, all of whom had grown up in a kind of ethnic limbo, belonging by heritage to a culture and homeland in which they were strangers, yet living and maturing in a culture that persisted in viewing them as Other, as alien and marginal. These writers incorporated their paradoxical condition—they were bicultural yet estranged from both cultures—into their poetry, fiction, and drama, producing a body of work that reflected a new Asian American voice that refused to mythologize ethnic origins or perpetuate stereotypes, yet avoided complete assimilation and in fact embraced difference on its own terms. For many of these writers, a crucial initiative of the decade was the attempt to redefine Asian American manhood and to counteract through their published writing what they perceived to have been the progressive cultural and psychological emasculation of the Asian male by the dominant culture.

Central to the activity of the 1970s was the work of a group called the Combined Asian Resources Project (CARP) whose members—Chin, Jeffery Paul Chan, Lawson Fusao Inada, Nathan Lee, Benjamin R. Tong, and Shawn Hsu Wong—actively sought publishing venues and performance spaces for the works of Asian American writers, created a collection of materials about those writers, found support for reissuing out-of-print works by the earliest Asian American writers, and sponsored literary conferences that focused on literary texts by Asian Americans. In addition, several valuable anthologies of writing by Asian Americans were published in the 1970s. The three best known of these anthologies are *Asian American Authors* (1972), edited by Kai-yu Hsu and Helen Palubinskas; *Aiiieeeee! An Anthology of Asian-American Writers* (1974), edited by CARP members Frank Chin, Jeffery Paul Chan, Lawson Fusao Inada, and Shawn Hsu Wong; and *Asian American Heritage: An Anthology of Prose and Poetry* (1974), edited by David Hsin-fu Wand.

Although these anthologies made some Asian writing more accessible to larger numbers of readers, Asian American literature had its first significant impact on the popular American consciousness in 1976 when Maxine Hong Kingston published *The Woman Warrior*, her rivetingly powerful memoir about growing up Chinese in America. Kingston's book was well-received in literary circles, winning the National Book Critics Circle Award for the best nonfiction of 1976, and paved the way for the young writers of the next decade to prove conclusively that the Asian American voice had a powerful resonance far beyond Chinatown or Little Tokyo or the neighborhood enclaves of Korean or Filipino immigrants. Unfortunately, Kingston was condemned by some Asian American writers who accused her of trying to "cash in" on the "feminist fad," of writing only for financial gain by creating "white-pleasing autobiography passing for pop cultural anthropology" (Kim 198). However, Kingston's detractors, although articulate and vocal, are few—limited mainly to a few male writers of Asian descent who have continued to argue that the tremendous sales and widespread popularity enjoyed by Asian American women writers undermines the masculinity of their male colleagues.

Kingston ushered in the 1980s with *China Men* (1980), winning the American Book Award. During that decade, Asian American writers earned recognition for the excellence and importance of their work. Among poets, Cathy Song won the Yale Series of Younger Poets competition for *Picture Bride* in 1982, Garrett Hongo was awarded the Lamont Poetry prize of the Academy of American Poets in 1987, and Li-Young

Lee was invited to read his poetry on National Public Radio. A new generation of playwrights graced the American stage: Genny Lim's *Island* (1985) was featured on National Public Television, and David Henry Hwang entranced Broadway audiences and won several Tony Awards for *M. Butterfly* in 1988. Into the growing market for and interest in Asian American writing came Amy Tan and *The Joy Luck Club* in 1989. The publication of that novel helped to catapult Asian American fiction into the literary mainstream when it appeared on national bestseller lists and became a featured book-club selection. By the end of the decade, many writers, including David Mura, Jessica Hagedorn, Philip Kan Gotanda, Ping Chong, Gish Jen, and Cynthia Kadohata discovered their work—along with that of Kingston and Tan—in textbook anthologies and on required reading lists for literature courses. Years later, the final pieces of evidence that Asian American writing has entrenched itself in the popular mind are the popular film versions of works by writers as diverse as Tan and Hwang, and memoir-writer Le-Ly Hayslip.

Partly because of the volume of their work and certainly because they write about subjects that resonate with so many mainstream readers, Chinese American women writers have been largely but inadvertently responsible for the new and sudden popularity of Asian American writing, a development that is made more startling because Chinese women were an almost invisible minority in American society until the early 1950s. Because most of them were kept out of the United States by laws specifically excluding Chinese women (including those who were married to American-born Chinese men) from immigration quotas, these women were outnumbered by Chinese men by approximately twenty to one. Given those numbers, we should not be surprised at the relatively small number of Chinese women writers in the first half of the twentieth century—in fact, we should be amazed that so many of the significant early Chinese American writers were women.

CHINESE AMERICAN WOMEN WRITERS

The earliest successful Chinese American women authors were the Eurasian sisters, Edith and Winnifred Eaton, daughters of an English artist and his Chinese wife. Although born in England, both Edith and Winnifred emigrated to the United States as adults, and it was as Americans that they began their writing careers. Despite their Caucasian features, the Eaton sisters used Asian pseudonyms: Edith became Sui Sin

Far, Cantonese for "Narcissus," and Winnifred became the faux-Japanese Onoto Watanna. The sisters' choices are intriguing, particularly because Edith decided to emphasize their Chinese heritage despite the Chinese Exclusion Act and widespread prejudice against the Chinese, while Winnifred, by contrast, assumed the more acceptable Japanese identity. During the decades before World War II, the Japanese enjoyed widespread respect in the United States, and Winnifred enhanced the prestige of her assumed identity by claiming that her mother belonged to a noble Japanese family from Nagasaki.

The Eaton sisters' writing paralleled their pseudonymous identities. As Sui Sin Far, Edith wrote in defense of the much maligned Chinese, taking up the fight against racism and injustice, attempting in her short stories to portray Chinese characters sympathetically and without resorting to prevalent stereotypes. Her ironic examinations of American culture are not limited to the plight of the Chinese immigrant; she also focuses attention on prejudice based on gender and class, or on that cultural phenomenon that she exemplified—the individual of mixed heritage who belongs neither to one culture nor to the other. Winnifred's career was markedly different from that of her sister. Onoto Watanna's "Japanese novels" were romances set in exotic Orientalized landscapes, featuring delicate, winsome Japanese women and influential powerful men—often white men—to whom the heroine must appeal for help or protection. Unlike Edith who used her pen as a weapon of protest, Winnifred's writing foregrounded and supported the status quo with its prejudices and cultural assumptions. So popular were Onoto Watanna's novels that they were translated into several European languages and went through several printings. They were adapted for the stage as well, and Winnifred eventually moved on to a highly successful career as a Hollywood scriptwriter.

Japan's attack on Pearl Harbor destroyed American readers' fascination with things Japanese, and created a new acceptance of the Chinese who were suddenly recognized as fellow victims of Japan's aggression. Several women—immigrants, American-born Chinese, American-raised Chinese—wrote novels and personal accounts about the devastating effects of the war on China, and about the strength and resilience of the Chinese people. Amy Ling points out that much of the war literature has a specifically defined purpose: "demonstration to the United States, a country superior in arms and supplies, that China was a worthy ally" ("Chinese American" 227). Among these writers were the three daughters of Lin Yutang—Adet and Anor, both of whom would have literary careers, and Mei-mei, the youngest and most Americanized. Also beginning their writing careers with personal accounts of the war were Han Suyin, Mai-mai Sze, and Helena Kuo. Although the war pieces received attention from readers who were chiefly concerned with discovering how the war was affecting some of America's Asian friends, it was Jade Snow Wong's *Fifth Chinese Daughter* that garnered the popularity and wide readership that the other works did not.

When the Exclusion Act was finally repealed in 1943, the increase in Chinese emigrating to the United States included significant numbers of women, and, as a result, the number of Chinese American women writers increased. Amy Ling and Elaine Kim, among others, have pointed out that despite the growing numbers of writers, Asian Americans' novels continued for a time to cater to the tastes of the predominantly white readership, looking with polite disfavor on Asian culture and enthusiastically embracing the American lifestyle.

There are two interesting exceptions to the tendency among early Asian writers in America to apologize for their ethnic backgrounds while commenting approvingly on Western culture. Han Suyin and Chuang Hua deserve mention for unapologetically examining the precarious balancing act performed by not only individuals who have both Asian and European or American blood but also Asians who are involved in interracial relationships. Herself of mixed blood, Han Suyin is a prolific writer with nearly two dozen titles—written over nearly half a century—in her oeuvre. Central to her most powerful novels are the problematic relationships between couples of different—and often antagonistic—ethnic and cultural backgrounds; and she underscores the tensions in such relationships by setting her novels in inherently contested territory that is unfamiliar to most of her readers. In Han Suyin's fiction, the cultural clashes involve Eurasian, American, Chinese, English, and Indian characters in settings as geographically diverse as Nepal, China under communism, and Hong Kong. Another writer, Chuang Hua, focuses her experimental novel, *Crossings* (1968), on life in that border country between cultures. Her protagonist, a Chinese woman who has grown up in England and the United States and spends time in France, falls in love with a European journalist, and their doomed affair is played out against the backdrop of the Korean War, which pits China and America against each other. Formally and structurally, Hua's novel is a forerunner of Maxine Hong Kingston's and Amy Tan's multiple genre approach to storytelling. In *Crossings*, the line of the narrative is ruptured time and again by autobiographical reminiscences, biographical elements, recounted dreams and nightmares, interior monologues, resulting in what Amy Ling calls "a highly original expression of the Chinese American hyphenated condition" (235).

As noted earlier, Maxine Hong Kingston's *Woman Warrior* took the American literary establishment as well as the reading public by surprise in 1975. In her text—which has been labeled variously talk-story memoir, autobiography, biography, novel—Kingston rejects the traditional linear fictional narrative structure, privileging instead a polyvocal mosaic of genres and styles that work together by both completing and contradicting each other, thus illustrating through content as well as form the collision between distinct and complex cultures. Writing about Kingston's work as the beginning of a new tradition in Asian American writing, Marlene Goldman points out that "Kingston's novel constitutes an alternative system for organizing experience, an activity directly related to the inscription of identity" (225). Kingston herself asserts that although *Woman Warrior* privileges women's circular narratives based on cultural memory and "old myths," the work itself is "much more American than Chinese" with characters who are "American people" (179). Indeed, the central theme in all of Kingston's writing is the attempt to sort out what being Chinese American means through the exploration of her experiences as an American-born child of immigrant parents.

By the time Amy Tan published her first novel, Maxine Hong Kingston had already introduced the general reading public to the talk-story narrative style. With her multiperspectival text, Tan was not only working in the traditions of her Chinese heritage and her Western training, but she also was following in the literary footsteps of a significant and powerful Asian American writer who had already begun to mine the rich vein of oral and written literary genres and traditions that exists within America's immigrant communities.

AMY TAN'S NOVELS

As a writer whose background includes Chinese tradition, Western Protestantism, American and Swiss education, experience in business writing, extensive readings in contemporary fiction, but more importantly the hyphenated condition common to all Americans of recent ethnic derivation, Amy Tan shares a number of common concerns and themes with other Asian American writers. Like them, she writes about the liminal identity of the hyphenated American, about the cultural chasms between immigrant parents and their American-born offspring and the linguistic gaps between generations, and finally about the need to discover a usable and recognizable past. But she does not write exclusively about the Asian experience, nor is her style specifically and wholly Asian despite its frequent allusions to traditional Chinese folk genres and its borrowings from the talk story tradition.

Writing in an experimental tradition that includes the works of James Joyce and William Faulkner, Louise Erdrich and Maxine Hong Kingston, Amy Tan constructs novels that explore critical issues by presenting multiple perspectives in parallel and intersecting narratives. Tan's three novels—*The Joy Luck Club*, *The Kitchen God's Wife*, and *The Hundred Secret Senses*—are textual collages, palimpsest narratives, stories that interrupt traditional linear narrative with interpolations of myth and fable, poetry and chant, autobiography and talk story, dreams, imaginings, and visionary tales.

Like Kingston, Tan employs her own brand of Chinese traditional talk story as a vehicle for exploring the lives of the mothers and daughters at the center of her novels. In an essay about Kingston and the Chinese oral tradition, Linda Ching Sledge provides a useful definition of talk story:

> a conservative, communal folk art by and for the common people, performed in the various dialects of diverse ethnic enclaves and never intended for the ears of non-Chinese. Because it served to redefine an embattled immigrant culture by providing its members immediate, ceremonial access to ancient lore, talk story retained the structures of Chinese oral wisdom (parables, proverbs, formulaic description, heroic biography, casuistical dialogue) long after other old-country traditions had died. (143)

In Tan's novels, talk story is the narrative strategy for those characters whose ties to Chinese tradition remain strong. In their attempts to explain their lives to their daughters, the mothers in *The Joy Luck Club* and *The Kitchen God's Wife* and Kwan in *The Hundred Secret Senses* draw on traditional oral forms to shape their stories and to disguise the urgency and seriousness with which they are attempting to transmit to their daughters (or a much younger sister in Kwan's case) the remnants of a culture that is fading even from their own lives. Evidence of the fragility of that culture lies not only in the jarring intrusions of Americanisms into the Chinese-English patois of the older generation, but more significantly in the fact that the stories of the younger generation are devoid of all but the faintest traces of an old world's oral literature. Those traces consist mainly of wispy recollections of stories and admonitory maxims heard in childhood and forgotten long since.

Talk story enables women who have been socialized into silence for most of their lives—the *Joy Luck* mothers, for instance—to reconfigure the events of those lives into acceptable public utterances: painful experiences are recast in the language of folk tale; cautionary reminders become gnomic phrases; real life takes on the contours of myth. More significantly, the act of performing talk story allows the storyteller to retain a comfortable distance between herself and her subject as well as between herself and her audience. Thus, the storyteller manages in some fashion to maintain the silence to which she is accustomed, as well as to speak out and share with others the important stories that have shaped her into the person that she is. For example Winnie Louie, who has hugged her dark secret to herself for a lifetime, acquires a strategy for unburdening herself of that secret, letting go of the past and finally gaining closure on the most painful period of her long eventful life.

Like the majority of American writers of recent immigrant ancestry, Amy Tan has a natural affinity for issues that are central to the lives of hyphenated Americans who must deal daily with several cross-cultural sets of expectations and experiences. In her work, Tan raises questions about the relationship between ethnicity, difference, gender, and identity. She writes about the diaspora culture as well as the many facets of biculturalism: cultural dislocation; the problems and challenges of integrating two cultures; intergenerational struggles within immigrant families; the conflict between acculturation and adherence to an ancestral tradition, and between assimilation and parochialism. She writes about the immigrant—and the second-generation American—as the embodiment of contested territory, cultural and political crossings, and questions of personal and national loyalties. Furthermore, Tan explores through her fiction the knotty issues of ethnic identity, more specifically the paradoxical nature of ethnic-American identity and biracial identity.

We should note, however, that Amy Tan does not confine herself to interrogations of the lives of ethnic Americans. In truth, although her fictional landscape is the geography of the immigrant her novels explore issues of familiar and universal interest: the common human struggle to establish a distinct identity; the search for roots and family connections; the tensions and bonds between generations, and related to that issue, the problematic yet richly influential relationship between mothers and daughters; the shape of women's lives in patriarchal cultures; and the need to connect past and present, present and future. Tan also writes about love and loss and redemption, about individuals coming to terms with the facts of their lives, and about the workings of fate in human existence. And in her novels, she celebrates bonding and connections, as well as family ties and friendships.

Drawing from traditional Chinese culture as well as contemporary Asian American and Chinatown culture, Amy Tan employs culturally specific figurative language and symbolism to entice her readers into the dual worlds of her novels, inviting them to explore with her the thorny issues that inform and shape her characters' lives. Through carefully deployed sensory stimuli—details, allusions, aural and visual motifs, image clusters, fragments of myth, linguistic wordplay—Tan alerts her readers to the multiple layers of meaning that reside in her prose. Among the most prevalent symbols, motifs, and archetypes in Tan's fiction are dreams, food, and clothing—and occupying an important position (albeit not always the center) in each novel is the crone, or wise older woman.

Dreams constitute a dominant motif in *The Joy Luck Club* and *The Kitchen God's Wife*, and become a major structural component in *The Hundred Secret Senses*. In Tan's novels, dreams are the connections between the conscious life and the unconscious, the bridges between worlds, the gateways to the self, and the representatives of deeply buried fears and personal monsters. In *The Joy Luck Club*, before she goes to China, June dreams repeatedly of arriving in Shanghai, telling her half-sisters that their mother is dead, and watching them run away from her in grief and anger. Dreams are also messages from the soul: ironic cautions against wishing for too much, or strategies for liberating the self and gaining happiness. As a young wife, Lindo Jong in *The Joy Luck Club* describes to her credulous in-laws a dream that she claims has revealed to her the inevitable tragedy that must come of her marriage. The terrified in-laws, anxious to protect their son, immediately pay Lindo for a divorce, hoping that by doing so, they can avert disaster. In *The Hundred Secret Senses*, Tan uses dreams to blur the lines between fantasy and reality, even suggesting that dreams represent memories of other lives in other places. Having listened for years to Kwan's stories in that drowsy period that comes just before true sleep, Olivia can no longer distinguish dream from story. As a child, Olivia "thought everyone remembered dreams as other lives, other selves" (28), and even after she goes to college, the dreams stay with her, indelibly etched into her imagination, shaping her life and her relationships.

Because dreams are so important in Tan's own life, some of her more memorable dreams, as well as those of her close friends, have inevitably been transmuted into fiction in the novels. A friend who dreamed of his own violent death repeatedly just before it became a tragic reality has been reincarnated in *The Kitchen God's Wife* as Gan, a young pilot who dreams about his own impending demise. Old Mr. Chou, a malevolent guardian of the dream world and the central figure in Amy Tan's childhood nightmares and fears, appears in *The Joy Luck Club* in Rose Hsu Jordan's recollections of dreams that frightened her so badly when she was a child that she tried hard not to fall asleep.

Food in Tan's three novels performs two basic functions: the realistic and the narrative. Through the realistic function, references to food situate the novel in a specific historical or seasonal time, or in an identifiable geographical or physical location. Tan, in *The Hundred Secret Senses*, neatly evokes an early morning market in Guilin by describing baskets of citrus fruit, dried beans, teas, chilis, food vendors frying pancakes in hot oil, live poultry in cages. In *The Kitchen God's Wife*, accounts of the lavish war-time meals prepared by Weili for her husband and his friends ironically call attention to the food shortages and starvation elsewhere in war-torn China. References to food also serve as narrative strategies. Celebratory feasts and special dinners bring characters together or introduce new characters, and they even create conflict or exacerbate existing tensions. *The Joy Luck Club* opens with the club members' first dinner together after the death of Suyuan Woo. At the meal, Suyuan's daughter June is introduced to the club as her mother's replacement and to readers as the central figure in the novel's framing narratives. After the meal, the aging club members drop a bombshell: they want June to go to China at their expense to find the half-sisters whom she has never met. The rest of the novel examines not only the motivations and hopes that have led the Joy Luck aunties to make this unusual request but also the emotions and insecurities that might lead June—or any of the other daughters—to refuse to go to China. Food also reveals a character's state of mind. Visiting Olivia after she and Simon have agreed to a divorce, Kwan is flummoxed by the emptiness of Olivia's refrigerator which contains only beer, pickles and other condiments, but no bread or meat or milk. The state of the refrigerator suggests that Olivia no longer cooks, and in fact has stopped having regular meals—quite possibly because she does not want to face the prospect of eating alone.

Clothing in Tan's novels has two major functions: to signify cultural confusions and collisions, and to signal concealment, subterfuge, or the performance of a feigned or manufactured identity. Characters who are unable to integrate their two cultures or who are experiencing some form of cultural dislocation tend to be recognizable in Tan's novels by the way they dress. Suyuan Woo arrives in the United States with no luggage save one trunk full of fancy silk dresses that are completely inappropriate to her new life, and she must resort to wearing one of only two much-too-large hand-me-down Western dresses. A photograph of Ying-ying St. Clair taken when she was released from Angel Island Immigration Station shows an Asian woman wearing a traditional ankle-length Chinese dress, oddly paired with a Westernized jacket constructed with padded shoulders, wide lapels, and large cloth buttons. The elements of Ying-ying's costume clash, East against West, providing a visual representation of the conflict in Ying-ying's own mind when she realizes that her husband has given her an American name and a new birth date. After years in America, Kwan still dresses like an immigrant. Annual family Christmas photographs show Kwan wearing bright summer clothes. "Everything about her is loud and clashing," Olivia remarks, adding that Kwan has a penchant for peculiar color combinations (*Secret Senses* 20). More complex are the instances in which a character dresses to perform a false identity. Traveling with her mother to live in Tientsin with her mother's protector, An-mei is startled one morning to find her mother dressed elaborately in Western clothing. An-mei, too, is hastily bundled into Western garb—a much-too-large ruffled white dress that resembles nothing she has ever worn. She later finds out that Wu Tsing, who owns the house where they will live, has a taste for imported luxuries "because foreigners had made him rich" (*Joy Luck* 223), and guesses eventually that her mother must wear the Western clothes to make Wu Tsing happy; by so doing, she will be able to keep her economic security. Jack Yee, likewise, has economic reasons for his masquerade—the overcoat that he finds, and wears as his own, contains money and immigration documents that enable him to travel to the United States. An-mei's mother publicly performs the role and wears the costume of the fashionable young third wife (and wears her Chinese widow's weeds in the privacy of her rooms) to ensure a secure financial future for her daughter; Jack, on the other hand, abandons his pregnant wife and infant

daughter in China when he leaves to seek his fortune—and he is condemned to live the rest of his life under an assumed name.

At the emotional center of Amy Tan's novels is the archetypal older
woman—the Crone or the Great Mother, as she sometimes is called—
who embodies the history of a family or a people, and holds within
herself the ancient wisdom and speech of her community. In myth and
religion, as in folklore and popular culture, the Great Mother represents
growth and fertility and nurturance, even as she also dominates and
overwhelms, possesses and devours. The Joy Luck mothers have borne
daughters, and invested in them all of the hopes and dreams that have
propelled the older generation across an ocean to America. To give those
daughters the best that the New World can offer, the mothers have sac-
rificed their youth and their homeland. And yet, the daughters see in
their mothers not nurturing angels, only stern disciplinarians, domi-
neering and possessive women who refuse to relinquish any maternal
control although the daughters are adults with their own homes. Like
the Joy Luck daughters, Pearl in *The Kitchen God's Wife* resents her
mother's power over her and feels overwhelmed by her mother, despite
the fact that for years they have lived some distance apart. Even *The
Hundred Secret Senses*, in which the only mother is flighty Louise Laguni,
has a Crone figure in Li Bin-bin, the aunt who raised Kwan after her
mother died in childbirth. Tan's Crones have had enormous influence
on the women whom they have raised to adulthood, nurturing on the
one hand and possessing on the other, encouraging and criticizing, giving love and withholding attention. The *Joy Luck* daughters and Kwan,
now grown women, still carry in their psyches the rejections and hurts
inflicted on them—they believe—by the women who dominated them
as children. Despite her good life in America, Kwan has always resented
the fact that Li Bin-bin sent her away from China without protest or
regret; and Kwan is impelled to visit China to show Li Bin-bin that she
has prospered. Significantly, the section of *The Joy Luck Club* in which
daughters and mothers achieve the beginnings of reconciliation is called
"Queen Mother of the Western Skies." The title has enormous significance, suggesting as it does that the daughters no longer view their
mothers as gorgons or harpies or devouring goddesses but rather as that
most exalted of the Great Mother's personas, the queen of heaven.

The fictional landscape that is frequently referred to as "Amy Tan
country" covers tremendous geographical territory over the span of decades and—in her third book—even centuries. In this landscape are
played out the oppositions between East and West, the conflict between

generations within a family, the clash between past and present. Tan's American locations exist within finite boundaries, in small sections of Oakland and San Francisco that, despite their narrow borders, encompass within them a multitude of cultures, ethnicities, and identities. Constantly threatened by encroaching Americanization embodied in the younger generation of inhabitants, these landscapes are connected with, yet different from, ancestral locations in a distant homeland. The place of origin is always China, in fact, a variety of Chinas: a country torn by the nineteenth-century T'ai Ping Rebellion, a nation ravaged by the Japanese army, a feudally stratified society, a gracious and privileged existence behind walls, or a culture uneasily embracing European goods while striving to maintain a Chinese way of life.

But Amy Tan country also is a landscape of the heart and the mind, and in Tan's novels the interior setting is as important as the physical locations of the novel's major events. Tan sets her novels within the circle of the Chinese American family and inside the minds and psyches of the family members; and she takes her readers into pre-Communist Chinese society in which the aristocratic family is the visible evidence of unwritten rules that require absolute filial piety, that sanction hierarchies based on gender and class, that condone concubinage and the virtual enslavement of women within arranged marriages, and that stress above everything else the importance of saving face rather than self. The interior landscapes are connected, for in Old China lie the seeds of the conflicts that threaten to rend the fragile bonds holding the immigrant family together; and only when the second generation recognizes and understands the ancestral landscape can the generational tensions be dissipated and replaced with genuine hope for a future that includes the family's entire heritage.

AMY TAN'S NOVELS AND THE ASIAN AMERICAN LITERARY CANON

Despite frequently being labelled an Asian American writer, Tan contends that Asian American issues—particularly Chinese American life—are not the primary driving force behind her writing. "I don't see myself writing about culture and the immigrant experience," she argues. "That's just part of the tapestry. What my books are about is relationships and family. I've had women come up to me and say they've felt the same way about their mothers, and they weren't immigrants" (Schleier 3).

During a public lecture at Barnard College in 1994, Tan told her audience of over a thousand listeners that the work of minority writers should not be labelled as ethnic literature because such labels prompt readers and critics to focus on the work solely as the manifestation of cultural or historical values or specific ethnic qualities. Tan suggested that literary works by minority writers be evaluated as literature rather than as cultural record ("Tan Argues Against Ethnic Literary Label"). Tan has spoken out elsewhere against the practice of ethnic labelling, maintaining that although Chinese culture forms the background and provides the settings for her novels, it is not necessarily what she writes about.

After she published *The Hundred Secret Senses*, Tan was once again questioned about her popularity as well as her possible identity as a role model for Asian Americans. In her response, she reiterated her opinion that ethnic writing should not be confined by its writers' geographical backgrounds:

> Placing on writers the responsibility to represent a culture is an onerous burden. Someone who writes fiction is not necessarily writing a depiction of any generalized group, they're writing a very specific story. There's also a danger in balkanizing literature, as if it should be read as sociology, or politics, or that it should answer questions like "What does **The Hundred Secret Senses** (boldface in original) have to teach us about Chinese culture?" As opposed to treating it as literature—as a story, language, memory. ("The Spirit Within")

Protest though she will, the inescapable fact is that although Tan's novels are indeed about universal concerns and commonly recognized themes, about relationships and familial bonds and self and identity, they also are about the members of an ethnic minority that has over a century or more developed a distinctive diaspora culture that exists within the larger framework of cultures that is known as the United States. Tan's fiction is ethnic in the sense that it is the product of the imagination of an author who is a second-generation Chinese American, a writer who is interested in and well-informed about the cultural, geographical, and historical borders of her life and that of her immigrant parents. In giving a voice to the immigrant community, Tan speaks for and to that community, reflecting its traditions and cultural structures, and articulating its values and its concerns.

Ultimately, we must say that Tan is an American novelist, and that the immigrant culture about which she writes is an important pattern in the great tapestry that is the United States, just as her novels are a strand in the web of twentieth-century American fiction. The fact that *The Joy Luck Club*, *The Kitchen God's Wife*, and *The Hundred Secret Senses* have become popular best-sellers suggests that Tan's fiction resonates for readers of all backgrounds; the proliferation of scholarly examinations of the novels points to the literary and cultural value of Tan's work.

Tan's writing career still is relatively new, and for that reason, a definitive assessment of her contribution to American literature is difficult to accomplish; however, if the number of master's theses and doctoral dissertations, professional journal articles, and book chapters written about *The Joy Luck Club* and even *The Kitchen God's Wife* is any gauge of literary merit, then Tan already has earned herself a berth in the canon of contemporary American literature. And certainly, *The Joy Luck Club* has become a staple of literature courses as well as conference papers and panel discussions. Tan's novels have proven both their literary staying power as well as their broad appeal to a wide readership, and it seems fair to predict that Tan will have a place in American literary history, not as an ethnic writer, but as an American writer who illuminates brilliantly and sensitively a distinctive and colorful aspect of the American experience.

3

The Joy Luck Club
(1988)

With the publication of her first novel, *The Joy Luck Club*, in 1988, Amy Tan became a household name. The book was a tremendous critical and commercial success from the beginning. Before the end of its first year, it had been named a selection for both the Book-of-the-Month Club and the Quality Paperback Club; foreign rights had been sold for Italy, France, Japan, Sweden, and Israel; serial rights went to the *Atlantic* magazine, *Ladies Home Journal*, and *San Francisco Focus*; and audio rights had been purchased by Dove.

The majority of reviews of *The Joy Luck Club* were strongly positive. *Publishers Weekly* called the novel "intensely poetic, startlingly imaginative and moving," describing it as "on the order of Maxine Hong Kingston's work, but more accessible, its Oriental orientation an irresistible magnet . . . a major achievement" (66). From the *Times Educational Supplement* came the following: "Amy Tan . . . is marvelously alert to the rich ambivalence in her material. With the delicacy of a butterfly she touches on matter that is ineradicable and profound" (19). Even less ebullient reviews acknowledged the fact that Tan's novel "strikes deep roots" (Pollard 44) and that readers "cannot help being charmed, however, by the sharpness of observation . . . and, finally, the universality of Tan's themes" (Koenig 82).

Structured as a series of personal narratives about eight women—four pairs of mothers and daughters—*The Joy Luck Club* chronicles the lives of its protagonists and traces the connections between the multiple cultures through which the women must negotiate their lives. The club of the title—a mah-jong-and-investment group formed by four Chinese immigrant women in the late 1940s—has met for over thirty years, and the novel opens shortly after the death of founding member Suyuan Woo. To correct an imbalance of players and to fill the empty East corner left by Suyuan at the mah-jong table, the three remaining members have asked her daughter, Jing-mei, to join them as her mother's replacement.

Significant differences are evident between the novel's two groups of women. Born in China and veterans of tremendous hardship and tragedy, the aging but still feisty mothers daily negotiate the significant events of their current lives through a minefield of memories of their youth in China, through stories of the pride and misery that marked their lives before their immigration to America. As immigrants, they have had to make significant changes in their lives; they have been forced to unpack their personal archives of pain and loss and to reassess their ambitions. Although outwardly they are well established in their new lives, the mothers never assimilate entirely; they never acquire fluent English, never relinquish the rituals and ceremonies of their pasts, and never forget their Chinese years. Their English-speaking daughters, by contrast, are thoroughly and indelibly American by birth, by education, and by inclination, their narratives turning on cross-cultural confusions, generational conflict, and questions of self and identity. Driven by resentment as well as fear of maternal disapproval, the daughters dismiss their mothers as Old World fossils, and they do not attempt to conceal their irritation with their mothers' stories about life in China. As the mothers struggle to imbue their daughters with a sense of Chinese tradition, the daughters in their turn wrestle with the need to reconcile their American lives and careers with the impossible and incomprehensible (to them) expectations of their mothers whose values remain rooted in China. The result is alienation and finally silence between mothers and daughters, exacerbated by an almost unbridgeable gulf between generations. The barriers between the women do not come down until the daughters learn to listen—truly listen—to their mothers' stories and begin to come to terms with the links between those stories and their own lives.

PLOT DEVELOPMENT

Amy Tan did not originally intend *The Joy Luck Club* to be a novel. The proposal that Tan had written and that Sandra Dijkstra had sold to Putnam was for a collection of short stories. The idea that the book might be a novel apparently did not occur to Tan until the publisher began planning the marketing strategy for the book. Thus the plot of *Joy Luck* develops through connections between stories, unfolding vignette by vignette, episode by episode, one anecdote or reminiscence at a time as the alternating and intertwined narratives of seven women who represent the immigrant generation and their American-born daughters. Providing continuity, coherence, and connection among the seven voices are the narratives of Jing-mei Woo, whose first appearance provides both context and background for the personal stories that follow.

Jing-mei's first narrative introduces the issues on which the novel focuses: the struggle for control between mothers and daughters; the daughters' bids for independent lives; the mothers' attempts to understand the dynamics of life in the New World and somehow to blend the best of their Old World culture with a new way of life that they do not comprehend. In subsequent chapters, Jing-mei more than any other narrator save Rose Hsu, reveals the connections between the narrators. In Jing-mei, the mothers' dreams and the daughters' concerns intersect; through Jing-mei's stories, all of the other stories find a context and an anchoring landscape.

The death of Suyuan Woo before the novel opens allows Amy Tan to show how the Joy Luck Club is forced to include in its ranks a member of the next generation. Jing-mei is catapulted into becoming the uneasy representative of the American-born daughters in a social ritual that is one of their mothers' last true links with a lost way of life on another continent. With Suyuan's death, the Joy Luck aunties are confronted with their own mortality, as well as with the fact that their daughters have grown into strangers. Suyuan has not had the opportunity to complete the account of her life story to Jing-mei, but the aunties still have time. In the weeks following Suyuan's death, each woman finds the power and the voice to speak the shaping events of her life to her daughter, and to acknowledge her pain and disappointment at her lack of rapport with her daughter; and each daughter in turn manages to articulate to herself—if not to her mother—the questions with which she wrestles, the frustrations she has been unable to voice, the small epiphanies that occur to her as she begins to understand her mother. And as each woman speaks, she contributes another layer to the palimpsest that is the novel's plot; she adds her voice to the collective narrative that drives the novel's forward motion.

NARRATIVE STRUCTURE

The Joy Luck Club essentially is episodic, with sections and chapters focusing on different protagonists whose individual stories create within the novel a series of climaxes that build toward the final narrative in which the stories come together. In the hands of a master storyteller like Tan, the episodic structure highlights the conflicts in the novel through a variety of structural devices: a changing, shifting focal point; clear relationships between cause and effect across time and great distance; cliffhangers and false resolutions and denouements that create suspense and tension. Each narrative stands alone, complete and self-contained, yet each narrative also is an essential pattern in the complex tapestry of the novel.

Tan has constructed her novel as a series of sixteen interlocking and interrelated narratives divided into four sections with four stories in a section. Each section is prefaced with a short fable or narrative proverb or vignette in which is distilled the essence of the stories that comprise the book; books and chapters are introduced with symbolic titles—pithy phrases, poetic words. Except for Suyuan who dies before the novel opens and Jing-mei whose voice opens two sections and closes two others, each character tells two stories about significant events or turning points in her life. "Feathers from a Thousand Li Away" reveals the mothers' early lives in distant China and describes the experiences that motivated their emigration to America. "Twenty-Six Malignant Gates," comprised of the daughters' stories, focuses on the emotional pain of their childhoods and their discontent as adults who are still unable to comprehend what their mothers want from them. "American Translation" continues the daughters' stories, foregrounding the American-born generation's struggle to accept their immigrant mothers as contemporary women instead of as outdated relics of a long-vanished alien way of life. And finally, all of the stories come together, West meets East, and mothers and daughters achieve a fragile detente in "Queen Mother of the Western Skies." Significantly, the two outer sections containing the mothers' stories enclose—and embrace—the two inner sections that testify to the daughters' emotional turmoil and their deep-seated fear that no matter what they accomplish, their mothers will find the achievements inadequate. Each section of the novel represents a definitive moment in four Chinese women's experiences as immigrants, or a significant stage in those women's relationships with their American-born daughters.

Jing-mei Woo, who tells the first story, introduces and elaborates the framing story that links all of the narratives. Structurally, her narratives lend shape and continuity to the novel, linking two generations of women. She alone of the eight women speaks four times, once in each section. Her voice opens the novel, introduces the dramatis personae, describes the Joy Luck Club, and sets in motion a series of crucial actions, revelations, and confessions; and, fittingly, she tells the concluding story in which rifts are healed and antagonists reconciled. Most important, she speaks for both herself and her recently deceased mother, and by telling Suyuan's story, by becoming, in fact, her mother's voice, Jing-mei bridges the chasm that divides the mothers from the daughters.

Jing-mei's description of the Joy Luck Club, its founding and long history, clarifies the connections among the novel's eight protagonists. For over three decades, the four members of the club have met in each others' homes to feast on Chinese dishes and play mah-jong. After the club decides to begin investing in selected stocks, the members' husbands and brothers join the regular meetings to enjoy the food and to participate in the financial discussions—but the mah-jong table is reserved strictly for the women. Throughout the club's long existence, the American-born daughters have by their own choice remained peripheral to the activity, attending meetings with their parents, dining on their mothers' specialty dishes, reluctantly babysitting the younger children, and silently criticizing their mothers for wearing traditional Chinese finery that is so elaborate as to be unfit for everyday Chinatown garb and too alien and unusual to pass for mainstream American party clothes.

Although the novel has seven speakers, no sense of fragmentation is evident. In fact, the clearest division is a simple bifurcation that separates one generation from another, mothers from daughters, a dislocation that is mirrored in the novel's structure that separates the mothers' stories from those of the daughters. Each generation is connected with the other by family ties and a shared racial identity; and each generation is estranged from the other through age and culture. Between the generations looms a series of nearly insurmountable barriers—time, experience, values, language—and the effect of the division is an image of antagonists poised for battle.

A powerful fable introduces the first section and thus the entire novel. In this tale, a duck who has ambitions to become a goose stretches out its neck so far that it turns into a swan—a bird that is too beautiful to be eaten. A woman purchases the swan, and together woman and bird travel across the ocean toward America and the woman's dreams. During the journey, the woman promises herself that life will be beautiful and different when she reaches her destination. In her dreams, once she is in America, she will bear a daughter who will resemble her physically but who will experience life far differently than she has. Unlike the woman, her daughter will never face discrimination or prejudice because she will be raised speaking only perfect American English. More important, the daughter will be privileged to have a life that is so rich in the advantages that America has to offer that she will always be "too full to swallow any sorrow" (17). Ultimately, the woman hopes to present her daughter with the swan—a gift that will be significant because the bird has exceeded its own ambitions and achieved a goal far greater than it had hoped to attain.

When the woman arrives in America, immigration officials confiscate her swan, leaving her only with a single feather as a reminder of the graceful companion that shared her journey, and obliterating her memory of why she has come to America. Eventually, the woman's dream is partially fulfilled: her daughter grows up speaking perfect English and "swallowing more Coca-Cola than sorrow" (17). But the rest of the dream remains elusive. Despite her desire and her diligence, the woman is unable to master English, and lacking a common tongue, mother and daughter find it difficult if not impossible to communicate with each other. In her old age, the mother is mute; linguistically, she is barred from telling the story of the duck-turned-swan, unable to present her daughter with the gift of the precious feather, yet still waiting patiently and now hopelessly for what now appears to be an impossibility—the magical day when she will have the ability to speak with her daughter in perfect American English.

The tale of the woman and the swan is a poignantly ironic introduction to the narratives that comprise the novel. In those stories are embedded the dreams and ambitions of immigrant women who have braved the unknown and travelled across oceans in the quest for a better life with limitless opportunities for their daughters. But the narratives prove only that daughters who can speak perfect American English and have never experienced genuine tragedy are strangers to their mothers whose Chinese tongues stumble over English words that they have never learned to pronounce. Unable to share with their daughters the stories of their own lives, the mothers must themselves swallow the sorrow and loneliness that their more fortunate daughters will never understand.

Regardless of the identity of the narrator, each of *Joy Luck*'s stories demonstrates the impact of the past on the present, reinforcing the notion that personal history shapes an individual's cultural identity and attitudes about the world. The mothers' lives are the consequences of difficult childhoods, war, poverty, starvation, and—in the case of Ying-ying St. Clair who alone had a privileged upbringing—a single traumatic childhood experience. Moreover, three of the mothers were married in their teens, two of them to men who did not appreciate them and one to a good man who was killed in the war; and one had children from her first marriage. For good or for ill, in a variety of ways, personal histories become the foundation on which the mothers build their new lives in America. In each story, the impact of the past on the present is clearly demonstrated. Each mother's Chinese past influences her American present; each daughter feels the impact of her own childhood on her adult life; and each mother's past affects her daughter's present. To complicate the equation, each mother has been influenced by her own mother's life. The past stretches back generation after generation, and—ironically—moves forward as well into the unseen future.

The mothers' stories have a number of common elements: dramatic recollections of girlhood and young womanhood in China, bewildered accounts of attempts to raise daughters in America, and almost dauntingly high expectations for their daughters. Likewise, the daughters' narratives display similarities: descriptions of their inability to meet their mothers' expectations, questions about the place of Chinese culture in their solidly American lives, and ignorance of the personal forces and private demons that drive their mothers. David Denby has pointed out that "each story centers on a moment of creation or self-destruction in a woman's life, the moment when her identity becomes fixed forever" (64). He is describing the film version of *The Joy Luck Club*, but his analysis applies equally well to the novel.

At the end of the novel, Jing-mei's concluding narrative functions in a number of ways as a paradigm for the other narrators' stories that need resolution. In traveling to China to meet her twin half-sisters—the now-grown babies for whom Suyuan had searched for almost forty years—Jing-mei brings closure and resolution to her mother's story as well as to her own. For Jing-mei, the journey is an epiphany and a discovery of self: finally aware of her mother's meaning, she is able to give voice to Suyuan's story as well as to the story that they share as mother and daughter. The Joy Luck aunties, whose gift of a generous check has sent Jing-mei on her pilgrimage to China, are well aware of the significance of the journey for her and for themselves. They beg her to tell her half-sisters about Suyuan—how she was able to create a full and rewarding life for herself in America, how she raised a family and gained success in her own way. The aunties encourage Jing-mei to make Suyuan come alive for her other daughters through narrative, through descriptions of her hopes and dreams, through re-creations of stories that she once told Jing-mei. Their words reveal their own dreams that in time their own daughters will, like Jing-mei, also remember and recount the stories their mothers have told.

In a Guangzhou hotel early in the visit to China, Jing-mei asks her father to recount to her the rest of the story of the twin baby girls, the story that Suyuan had not had the opportunity to finish telling her. During that late night conversation, Jing-mei also learns that her Chinese name—the name that her mother gave her when she was born, the name that she once repudiated in favor of the more American sounding June—represents her mother's past and present, losses and hopes. Jing-mei means "younger sister who [is] supposed to be the essence of the others" (281). For Suyuan, her American daughter would be the replacement child who would enable Suyuan to bear the loss of the twins. In going to China, then, to meet her older sisters, Jing-mei reconciles Suyuan's two lives, two cultures, two countries; she reconciles her self with her mother; and she gives the aunties the hope that they, too, will be reconciled with their daughters.

POINT OF VIEW

The stories that stitch together the fabric of *The Joy Luck Club* are told by first-person narrators, by the individuals to whom those stories happened. Each narrator performs as both protagonist and peripheral observer—the central figure in her own story, and a supporting character in others' stories—thus providing the novel with a richly textured collective point of view not generally possible with a single character who functions simply as the sole narrator. Like all first-person narrators, however, each *Joy Luck* storyteller has the predictable limitations of all human beings, and her knowledge is therefore limited to what she has directly experienced and seen—what she can realistically know. Being human, first-person narrators can be unreliable, and they can misinterpret events, withhold information, editorialize, and inadvertently mislead. After Suyuan's death, Jing-mei recalls that she and her mother frequently misunderstood each other; they each interpreted the other's meaning so differently that Jing-mei heard far less than her mother meant while Suyuan tended to invest what she heard with considerably more significance than her daughter ever intended.

Addressing their stories to their daughters, the mothers remain aware that their words are falling on indifferent ears; nevertheless, they persevere, hoping that a fragment of thought or a phrase will resonate in the heart of a daughter who will cherish the nugget of wisdom and pass it on to her own daughter. "It's too late to change you," Lindo Jong says to Waverly, adding that the only reason for the advice is concern for Waverly's child who might grow to adulthood knowing nothing of her double cultural heritage (49). The mothers' stories are carefully selected from vast reservoirs of memories and offered to the daughters as gifts of the heart, offerings of the soul, talismans to help the younger women confront their problems, secure in the knowledge that they have the strength of mothers, grandmothers, and great-grandmothers behind them. The mothers occasionally speak only in their minds, formulating questions, answers, thoughts that they cannot express to their daughters; but Ying-ying alone of the mothers speaks to herself only, having long since lost all rapport with her daughter who at birth "sprang from [her] like a slippery fish and has been swimming away ever since" (242). Ying-ying's narratives, addressed to herself, reveal a woman in the process of rediscovering her self after decades of numbness caused by early pain. Not until she has reclaimed her past and her spirit will she be able to speak openly about her first disastrous marriage to a daughter who is suffering through the pain of a failed marriage.

None of the daughters speaks directly to her mother through her story. These second-generation Chinese-American women are convinced that their mothers are irrevocably disappointed in them; and certain that nothing they do will ever win maternal approval or praise—and they are hesitant to confess to their mothers the stories of their insecurities, their failed relationships, their fears about the future. In their narratives—shaped as internal monologues—the daughters document the emotional and psychological conflicts with which they wrestle daily, and they give voice to their emotional estrangement from their mothers to whom they dare not say what is truly in their hearts.

The sixteen stories that comprise the four sections have a cumulative power that underscores the tragedy of the women's misunderstandings and highlights the comedy in the familial relationships that bind them one to another. But those sixteen stories also demonstrate the power of memory and the imagination to preserve the past or to reshape it. Early in the novel, as she attempts to recall everything that Suyuan has said about the original Joy Luck Club, Jing-mei acknowledges the fictionality of her mother's stories, saying that she had always believed her mother's tales about the war years in Kweilin to be little more than some sort of Chinese fairy tale because the conclusion differed slightly with each re-telling, and the story constantly expanded and became more elaborate with time. Thus, Jing-mei is surprised when one evening, Suyuan tells the Kweilin story again, but with a completely different ending that bears no resemblance to the earlier versions. That new ending turns out to be the truth—as much of the truth as Suyuan believes Jing-mei can understand at that point in their relationship. And because Suyuan dies before she is able to retell the story with its complete and unaltered conclusion, Jing-mei must go to China to discover how the Kweilin story really ends (a conclusion that Suyuan has been denied), and to learn about the hidden years of Suyuan's life.

CHARACTER DEVELOPMENT

At the heart of *The Joy Luck Club* are the four mothers whose lives are the sites of the intersection of past and present, China and America, mother and daughter. Having fled from China in the 1940s and created good lives for themselves in an alien land, these women are, nevertheless, still more Chinese than they are American. They share a common concern that their daughters, now grown to womanhood knowing little about their mothers or their mothers' homeland, will have nothing of the ancestral homeland and culture to pass on to their children. Concealing her emotions behind an unsentimental and no-nonsense facade, each mother has a story that she longs to share with her daughter—and each tale reveals the trauma of a long-ago pivotal event that transformed a naive young girl into a self-directed woman who has learned to rely on and trust only herself.

Initially, Jing-mei gives the impression that her Joy Luck aunties are nearly indistinguishable, generic, elderly Chinese immigrants. Describing their dress at her first club meeting as a mah-jong player, she creates the picture of three aging women wearing nearly identical outfits of pants, brightly colored print blouses, and athletic shoes. And indeed, as has already been mentioned, strong similarities do exist among the women of that generation: they all have lived painful and tragic lives in China and have come to the United States for a second chance at life; they are ambitious for their children and completely baffled by the daughters in whom they have put all of their hopes.

Suyuan Woo appears in the novel as an absence, as the subject of her daughter's first narrative. During World War II, Suyuan is forced to leave her twin baby girls beside a road in the hope that someone stronger than she will find them and care for them. In their clothes, she has concealed money and jewelry along with their names and the address of Suyuan's family home. She collapses shortly thereafter, and while in the hospital she learns that her husband is dead. Later marrying a man whom she meets while she is ill, Suyuan and her new husband search for the babies but discover only that her home has been obliterated by the Japanese bombs and that there is no trace of the babies. In 1949, the couple emigrate to the United States where their daughter Jing-mei is born. Although for years she continues to search for her twin daughters by writing to friends in China, Suyuan never sees the twins again, and lives out the rest of her life feeling the absence of those babies and desperately attempting to discover their fate.

An-mei Hsu introduces herself through her reminiscence about a grandmother who refuses to tell An-mei about her mother who has gone away, leaving the child in the grandmother's care. When the grandmother falls ill, An-mei's mother returns to care for her, but the grandmother dies, and An-mei goes to live with her mother in Tientsin. Gradually and indirectly, An-mei discovers that her mother has been forced to become a rich man's concubine and to bear him a son who is taken away to be raised by the man's most powerful wife. Carefully timing her act to bring the greatest possible benefit to her children, An-mei's mother commits suicide, and the rich man, fearful of her ghost, promises to raise An-mei as his own child.

Lindo Jong is betrothed to Tyan-yu, a neighbor's son, when she is two years old, goes to live with her future in-laws at twelve, and is married at sixteen. The marriage is a disaster from the beginning: few guests attend the wedding because of the war, her immature husband does not desire her, and her mother-in-law's demands for a grandchild escalate.

Craftily playing on her in-laws' superstitions, Lindo maneuvers the family into releasing her from the marriage and providing her with sufficient money to emigrate to America to build a new life for herself. In her adopted country, she marries Tin Jong and bears three children, including her daughter Waverly.

Ying-ying St. Clair grows up wealthy, surrounded with luxury, and spoiled. At sixteen she enters an arranged marriage. She falls in love with her husband, only to discover after she becomes pregnant that he is a womanizer. When he leaves her for an opera singer, she has an abortion and then exiles herself to an existence with poor relations for ten years. Clifford St. Clair ardently courts Ying-ying for four years, but she refuses to accept his proposal of marriage until after she hears that her former husband is dead. To her surprise, Ying-ying loses a part of herself with the death of the man she has loved: "I willing gave up my *chi*," she says, referring to her spirit, her essential self, her personality and distinctive identity. Significantly, Ying-ying is the only narrator who speaks solely to herself, recounting the story of her life in an interior monologue through which she seeks to rediscover her *chi* and reconnect with the woman she once was.

Doggedly clinging to their memories of life in China even as they adapt to American culture, the mothers deliberately remain suspended between two worlds and two cultures, embracing—as they believe—the best of each world and creating a new way of life that they hope to pass on as their legacy to their children. But Lindo Jong speaks for all of the mothers when she recalls wistfully that she once dreamed of giving her children the best of their two heritages: "American circumstances and Chinese character." And she adds sadly, "How could I know these two things do not mix?" (254). As they grow older, the mothers grow more and more aware that they have—despite their best efforts—raised completely Westernized children. The ancestral culture has proved to be almost powerless against the domination of the culture of the New World.

The daughters are noticeably more American than Chinese despite their clearly Asian features, and since childhood, they deliberately have attempted to cultivate American ways and repudiate much of their Chinese heritage. Now adults, they have no patience with their elderly mothers whose daily communication still is conducted in Chinese and whose English at best remains a fractured version of the American lingua franca. The daughters yearn for an Americanization that they can neither define nor describe. More than anything else, they are unhappy and unfulfilled; for some reason, they often feel inferior to their mothers and unworthy of the maternal ambitions that have defined and in some cases scarred their childhood and adolescent years.

Jing-mei Woo, known as June among her contemporaries, is thirty-six years old and still entrapped by her mother's long-ago dream of an accomplished and famous daughter. As a child she was forced to study the piano because her mother wanted to have a talented child about whom to brag, but after a disastrous talent show performance and an angry exchange of words between mother and daughter, Jing-mei never again touches the piano. Still, her mother's disappointment follows her into adulthood, and Jing-mei continues to dwell on what she considers to be her failures—she was never a straight-A student, she did not attend Stanford University, she dropped out of school without earning her baccalaureate degree. Now that Suyuan is gone, Jing-mei no longer has a chance to win her mother's approval or to live up to her mother's expectations. Worse than that, she has never developed the courage to speak with her mother about her own need to decide on a course of action for herself, and she has never asked Suyuan why her ambitions for her daughter were so grand that Jing-mei could never be successful. Now in her late thirties, Jing-mei continues to be paralyzed by tremendous doubts about her abilities; she is insecure and unsure of her worth as a person.

Waverly Jong is Jing-mei's opposite: a childhood success and a brash, confident young woman on her way to the top. As a child, she becomes famous as "Chinatown's Littlest Chinese Chess Champion." As an adult, she is a tax lawyer and the mother of four-year-old Shoshana—and she is loved by kind, romantic Rich Schields. Yet Waverly is unhappy: she fears her mother's penchant for negative commentary and dismissive remarks about issues and concerns of great importance to Waverly—and anticipating her mother's criticism, she cannot seem to summon the courage or the words to announce the plans for her impending marriage to Rich.

After several years of marriage, Lena St. Clair is angry and bitter. She has helped her husband, Harold, establish a successful architectural firm, but she feels that he has never valued her contributions to the partnership or the marriage—and she finds herself groping for ways to describe their problems that are so complicated and deeply rooted that she cannot articulate them. In her heart, Lena is convinced that somehow she deserves her dysfunctional marriage to Harold because a chance remark from her mother years before had led the young Lena to hate a neighbor boy so much that she wished him dead. To Lena, Harold represents retribution, a punishment with which she must live to atone for teenage hatred.

Rose Hsu Jordan, the only one of the daughters who has taken her husband's name, is a timid uncertain woman whose fifteen-year marriage to Ted Jordan ends abruptly when he leaves her. Her indecisiveness—the result of childhood nightmares brought on by her mother's stories—paralyzes her, and she finds it nearly impossible to make decisions related to the divorce.

Despite their superficial differences, the daughters share a common and significant characteristic: whether they have listened carefully when their mothers spoke about the past, their childhoods have been shaped by their mothers, deeply marked by their mother's stories. At some subconscious level, the daughters recognize their mothers' influence and understand the strength of the bonds that link them to their mothers. Resenting their inability to break away completely from what they perceive to be maternal control, they distance themselves from their mothers by withholding information about their personal lives, by living as far away from Chinatown as they can afford, and by marrying out of the Chinese community.

Ying-ying St. Clair plaintively articulates the cultural separation between herself and her daughter Lena: ''All her life I have watched her as though from another shore'' (274). Ying-ying's allusion to the ocean separating mother and daughter is not just a figure of speech but an essential truth about all of the mothers and their daughters. Emotionally, the mothers are still in pre-war China on the other side of the Pacific Ocean, whereas to their American-born daughters, China is a foreign country that they have never seen and about which they know little. China, for the younger women, merely is a shadowy setting of their mothers' stories, an intangible geography for narratives that have—in their telling—taken on the aura of dark fairy tales.

SETTING

Although Jing-mei's framework narrative is set in California in the 1980s, *The Joy Luck Club* takes in considerable temporal and geographical territory, from post-feudal China to war-time China, to the America of the 1950s, to modern China under communist domination. But setting in Tan's novel represents far more than a simple series of locations for significant events; setting in *Joy Luck* provides an atmospheric backdrop that emphasizes the sense of cultural disjunction that pervades the stories.

China as it appears in stories told by the mothers is a mysterious country, feudal and oppressive, yet strangely beautiful and colorful. Old China is first mentioned in a story that Jing-mei remembers hearing her mother tell. In that story, Suyuan describes Kweilin, a region famous for its beauty, a place that has been immortalized in silk paintings and poetry. Jing-mei remembers dreaming of jagged mountains rising above a winding river bordered by green mossy banks, and she recalls that when she finally saw Kweilin, she realized that her dreams were paltry imaginings that in no way resembled the magic beauty of the real mountains and river. Ying-ying's childhood also is spent in that dream China, which she recreates through images of porcelain and jade, lanterns in the trees and garden pavilions. The Moon Festival that is central to her narrative is a blur of gaudily decorated boats on a lake, servants preparing baskets of food, the sound of cicadas and crickets and frogs, the Moon Lady's wailing song rising into the night over the music of flutes and drums. By contrast, Lindo's China is a feudal society, seen through the eyes of a girl from a family of modest means. When she goes to live with her future in-laws in their huge compound with many courtyards and houses with several levels, Lindo becomes a glorified servant as she is put to work learning how to cook, do the laundry, mend torn clothing, even clean chamber pots. As the child of a rich man's concubine, An-mei lives in Ying-ying's world of luxury and comfort, but because of her mother's position, she is marginal to the household and is thus able to view objectively the domestic hierarchy that excludes her and her mother, and she remains aware—as Lindo does—that she is an outsider.

Perhaps because they are recreated through memory, the Chinese settings seem slightly unreal, very much like artfully planned and executed stage settings. This sense of careful design enhances Tan's portrayal of traditional China with its rigidly structured hierarchies and social structures, its codified rituals, and its established protocols governing the lives of its people. By contrast, the American settings pulse with life, energy, and chaos. Whereas in China, the Joy Luck mothers had centuries of established convention dictating their behavior, America's cultural practices are strange and unfathomable—and these women, who have left China specifically for the chance to start afresh in a new country far from the stultifying tradition of the old, find themselves reverting to the familiar customs of their faraway homeland. Barred for a variety of reasons from achieving the dreams of success that brought them to America, the mothers transfer their ambitions to their daughters in whom they hope to combine the best of Chinese and American culture. On those daughters, who grow up in Chinatown but attend American schools, rest the hopes of their immigrant mothers.

In the novel—as in reality—Chinatown combines elements of the ancestral homeland that the mothers have left with the essence of America, the country in which they have created new lives. Tan's Chinatown is the bustling landscape of the Chinese immigrant community, a mosaic of sights and sounds, a concatenation of aromas and flavors that bring to life a place that simultaneously is American and exotic. In this Chinatown are a medicinal herb shop, the Ping Yuen Fish Market and the China Gem Company, Hong Sing's cafe with a menu in Chinese only, a printing business that produces traditional gold-embossed wedding invitations and festive red celebration banners.

Within the homes of the Joy Luck Club members, the distinctly Chinese atmosphere is evoked in odors. The Hsus' house is permeated with the lingering odors of countless Chinese meals prepared in the inadequate kitchen, with the stale memories of once fragrant smells now faintly masked by the inevitable film of grease resulting from years of frying and sautéing. Waverly Jong recalls growing up in a small flat located on the floor above a Chinese bakery that specialized in a variety of delicacies intended for dim sum. She remembers that every morning the aroma of fried sesame balls and curried chicken pastries wafted into the Jong flat from the bakery below.

Although Chinatown is—as its name suggests—an outpost of the old country set incongruously in the heart of California, the distinctly Chinese ambiance is punctuated by intrusions of Western culture. Dominating weekend activities in Chinatown is the First Chinese Baptist Church, the setting for the annual neighborhood Christmas party at which local children are given gifts donated by parishioners of churches outside Chinatown. Also in Chinatown are several American institutions: a McDonald's restaurant with a large sign flaunting Chinese characters that unaccountably represent the words, "wheat," "east," and "building"; the Bank of America; Pacific Telephone; and a fortune-cookie factory.

From their earliest years, the children of Chinatown are aware that they live on the border between two worlds. They suck on Life Savers candy while waiting for their dinners of steamed dumplings, they learn to play the piano from elderly Chinese immigrants who teach them selections by Grieg and Schumann, and they attend church-sponsored

Christmas parties that feature a Chinese man in a paper and cotton Santa Claus costume. Perhaps tiring of the constant need to negotiate their way between two seemingly irreconcilable cultures, after they become adults the children choose the American way of life and discard their childhood Chinese names. Leaving behind their old ethnic neighborhoods, they take up residence in Victorian houses in white districts like Russian Hill and Ashbury Heights, or they move out into the country, into trendy converted barns with postmodern details—structures that bear no resemblance to the crowded walk-up Chinatown apartments of their childhoods.

LITERARY DEVICES

To create texts that both tell stories and permit readers to construct meaning, novelists rely on a wide range of literary devices that function as individual elements or signs of a highly compressed and densely sensual literary language. Among the most common of these devices are symbols (which can be objects, persons, places, events, among others), icons, allusions, image clusters, motifs, archetypes, and linguistic patterns—all of which, in a work of fiction, contribute to the texture and richness of the work by engaging a reader's senses along with the reader's mind.

The Joy Luck Club is dense with symbols and allusions, and interwoven with icons and motifs, that involve the Joy Luck Club, food, and the Chinese language and Chinese-English patois, as well as mirrors, celebrations and events, home interiors, and dreams. Through these devices, Tan explores the layers of the palimpsest that is her text, her narrative of the immigrant experience in America, her exploration of the bond between mother and daughter.

A crucially important symbol in the novel is the Joy Luck Club with its mah-jong table as a centerpiece that links past and present, and codifies place and identity for club members. During the war years in Japanese-occupied China, Suyuan Woo had founded the first incarnation of the club for herself and a handful of other young women, all refugees from the relentlessly advancing Japanese army. While it existed, the club was a gesture of defiance that allowed the women to briefly forget the terrors and privations of wartime China by meeting weekly to celebrate the fact that they were still alive and to play mah-jong seriously. Remembering always that a war was laying waste to the China of their

girlhoods, and constantly aware that giving in to despair was tanta-
mount to wishing for everything that was already gone, Suyuan and her
friends held the war at bay by using the meager food supplies to prepare
symbolic dishes that were traditionally credited with bringing good fortune. Feasting on the carefully prepared delicacies and then gathering
around Suyuan's special mah-jong table, they played and talked and
shared stories about happier times before the war. The fate of the original
Joy Luck Club is unclear; whenever Suyuan told Jing-mei the story of
the club, she changed the ending. But ultimately, the club is impotent
against the juggernaut of war, and when the fighting and the bloodshed
finally end, Suyuan finds herself widowed and childless.

When, in 1949, Suyuan forms the new Joy Luck Club in San Francisco,
she recreates a memory, a reminder of her indomitable younger self, and
provides herself with a link to the life that she has left, with the homeland that she will never see again. For three decades, she and her fellow
immigrants, An-Mei Hsu, Lindo Jong, and Ying-ying St. Clair, meet to
play mah-jong, indulge in a cooking rivalry, and tell stories—the same
stories about China repeated over and over until those stories take on
the outlines of myth and legend.

As important as the Joy Luck Club is to the immigrant mothers, their
daughters find its existence perplexing and embarrassing. Jing-mei
points out that as a child she considered the club to be some sort of
shameful Chinese secret society, on a par with the Ku Klux Klan or the
clandestine dances of television Indians preparing for battle. None of the
other daughters mention the club or their mothers' participation in it;
but only through the intervention of the Joy Luck Club aunties are the
daughters, represented by Jing-Mei, able finally to hear their mothers'
stories, to reconcile the two disparate worlds of their heritage, and to
receive symbolically the gift of the swan feather. When Jing-mei takes
her mother's place on the East side of the mah-jong table, she begins her
journey east—to China where the stories began—and through her the
circle of mothers and daughters is closed and completed.

Food imagery plays a significant role in each separate narrative of the
novel, linking past and present and future, bonding families and generations, expressing community—and providing a linguistic code that
facilitates the retrieval of personal histories from oblivion. Food allows
mothers to communicate with their daughters in a common language;
food is an emotional homeland for both generations.

From the first narrative, Tan establishes the links between generations
and between families through food. As Jing-mei readies herself to be-

come a member of the Joy Luck Club, she recalls that her mother had been scheduled to host the meeting that Jing-mei is about to attend. Because Lindo Jong had served red bean soup at a previous club dinner, Suyuan, in the spirit of the culinary rivalry between the club members, had intended to prepare black sesame-seed soup for the club members. Although the club's purpose is to play mah-jong and to discuss the group's investments, the activity at the center of club meetings is eating, communal dining accompanied by storytelling and good-natured arguing. When, at the end of the novel, Jing-mei finally visits the country of her mother's birth, another symbolic meal brings her father's family together. For their first meal together, Jing-mei, her father, and his ancient aunt and her family dine on hamburgers, french fries, and apple pie with ice cream. Jing-mei's first dinner in China is American fast food, provided by room service.

Food imagery enables the mothers to find words to describe their history. When Lindo Jong tells the story of her first unfortunate marriage, her account is larded with references to food: she meets her betrothed at a red-egg ceremony celebrating his naming; she is relegated to the kitchen to chop vegetables when she goes to live with her in-laws; she learns to cook Tyan-yu's favorite dishes. After the wedding, Lindo personally sees to her husband's breakfast every morning and cooks a special eight-ingredient tonic soup for his mother's evening meal. Ying-ying St. Clair's memory of a Moon Festival celebration of her childhood is similarly laced with food references. Interspersed with Ying-ying's narration of the events of the picnic are explicit descriptions of the food that has been packed by the servants for the picnic meal: sticky rice cakes wrapped in lotus leaves; luxury fruits like apples, pomegranates, and pears; and a selection of preserved meats and vegetables. These descriptions are juxtaposed with her recollection of a woman cleaning fish, butchering chickens, and cooking freshwater eels. Although Ying-ying now lives in California, the foods of her Chinese childhood are integral elements of the story of her life.

For An-mei Hsu, food is a reminder of pain that she associates with her grandmother whom she called Popo. As a four-year-old child, An-mei is badly scalded on her neck when a pot of steaming soup tips off a table onto her, and Popo nurses her through the nights of pain by pouring water to soothe the burned skin so that little An-mei can go to sleep. Another memory takes her to Popo's deathbed beside which An-mei's mother is concocting a special restorative soup with herbs and medicines. As the child watches, her mother cuts a piece of flesh from her own arm and drops the piece into the soup, invoking an ancient magical charm in an attempt to heal the dying Popo. Forever after, An-mei considers her mother's action to be an example of the proper way for a woman to honor her mother.

Because food can be so culturally specific, it functions to emphasize differences between generations, between cultures. When Waverly brings her fiancé Rich to dinner at her parents' home, his unawareness of the nuances of behavior required by the Jongs' culture is revealed in his performance at the dinner table. "I couldn't save him" (177), laments Waverly before she proceeds to outline his mistakes: he drinks too much of the wine that he has brought to the teetotaling Jongs; he helps himself to generous portions of shrimp before anyone else has had a bite; he does not taste politely every dish that is offered; and he pours soy sauce liberally over a special dish on which Lindo Jong prides herself. Sadly, although Waverly knows that Rich has appalled her parents and possibly offended their sensibilities, Rich believes that he has done well, and when he and Waverly return to their apartment, he crows delightedly that he and her parents have certainly impressed each other favorably. Like Rich, Waverly's daughter, Shoshana, reveals her ignorance of Chinese culture and polite behavior at the dinner table. Invited to a special New Year crab feast at the Woos' house, Shoshana waits until Waverly has carefully selected for her the largest, plumpest crab on the platter before whining to the assembled dinner guests that she hates crab.

The crucial role played by language—a third significant narrative device—is introduced early in *The Joy Luck Club*, embedded in the fable about the swan that serves as prologue to the first section of the novel. Integral to the fable is the woman's dream of a daughter whose only language is perfect American English; but equally central is the woman's silence because she has not mastered English. As Jing-mei points out more than once, she and her mother did not communicate in the same language; Jing-mei spoke to her mother in English, and Suyuan invariably responded in Chinese. Lacking a shared language and a common cultural tongue, Tan's mothers and daughters face each other across the communication barrier that not only divides generations but also separates the old world and the new, the immigrant and the American-born.

To the frustration of the younger Americanized generation, the immigrant generation has created its own speech, a patois that incorporates Chinese and English words in a syntax that is derived from both languages and produces rich meanings of its own. For example, the widowed Ying-ying obliquely describes her straitened circumstances with a casual reference to her "so-so security" that her daughter supplements with a monthly check (243). Jing-mei complains about the special language used by the Joy Luck aunties who speak partly in broken English, partly in Chinese. The Chinatown patois bonds the mothers even as it confuses, alienates, and excludes their daughters who become impatient when their mothers speak Chinese, or smirk with superiority when their mothers caution that speeding causes unnecessary "tear and wear" on automobiles (150), or complain about a child who is a "college drop-off" (37). But for the mothers, the hybrid tongue is a form of self-identification, a means of inscribing their unique existence on a culture that continues to exclude them, a strategy for preserving their heritage even as they embrace a new life.

Language becomes a political issue. Acutely aware that power and position in American culture are determined in large part by an individual's ability to speak correct English with one of the approved accents, the mothers create their own private hierarchy within their circle, privileging the Chinese language. And although they are mired in an invisible ethnic ghetto to which their daughters have consigned them, and powerless because they lack skill in the dominant tongue, the mothers—who are bursting with stories to share and emotions to express—use Chinese and their special patois to articulate their most important thoughts, to exclude those whom they wish to ignore, to speak in their own authentic voices. When she gives Jing-mei a jade pendant, Suyuan lapses into Chinese, the language of her heart, to reveal that she has worn the pendant next to her skin so that when Jing-mei wears the piece she will understand her mother and realize at last what truly is important in her life. For Ying-ying St. Clair, Chinese represents her true self, the Ying-ying who has been erased by an unfaithful first husband, by a too-protective second husband who changed her name and birth date when she emigrated to America and now insists on speaking for her, interpreting her every comment to fit neatly into his image of her. After her second child—a boy—is stillborn, Ying-ying refuses to mention the baby in English, speaking only in Chinese so that her husband is forced to ask their daughter what her mother means. In that way, Ying-ying manages to separate a part of herself from the overwhelming, engulfing affection of her husband.

For the mothers, the Chinese language and the Chinatown patois enable a subversive form of humor at the expense of those who are not privy to the nuances of either tongue. A few examples should suffice. On a visit to her architect daughter's new house—a renovated barn with a trendy minimalist interior—reticence prevents Ying-ying from openly criticizing a house that she dislikes because its furnishing and ornaments are all for ostentatious display, for making a statement rather than for beauty. But slyly claiming that she cannot pronounce accurately the word that names her daughter's profession, Ying-ying contrives to voice her true opinion when she labels Lena—and by extension, her house—"arty tecky" (243), a phrase that wittily conveys judgment and dismissal. Ying-ying gives in to the same impulse that prompts An-mei Hsu to ask her daughter, Rose, why she needs to talk with a "Psyche-atricks" about her failing marriage. An-mei's opinion is clear: therapy is nothing but a method for playing tricks on the mind.

MAJOR THEMES AND ISSUES

Although she writes about Asian immigrants in California's ethnic neighborhoods and highlights culture-specific issues in her novels, Amy Tan has earned praise and her loyal international readership for her treatment of universal themes—recurrent subjects or topics that resonate deeply for readers of all ages and backgrounds. Chief among the themes that have been identified in *The Joy Luck Club* by readers and critics is the mother-daughter dyad and its inherent conflicts and frictions; but equally important issues are self-discovery and the search for identity, the search for the American Dream, acculturation and ethnicity (and by extension, cultural alienation), the disintegration of family relationships, and separation and loss. Through her portrayal of the four mother-daughter pairs in *Joy Luck*, Tan explores the generational dynamics that function in the relationship between mother and daughter, and the influence of the remembered relationship between a mother and her own mother.

The major source of friction between Tan's mothers and daughters is the mothers' desire for their daughters to be successful by American measures while remaining culturally Chinese. Now that the daughters are grown women with lives of their own, the mothers have been forced to admit to themselves that their dreams will more than likely never find fulfillment, but their legacy of maternal ambition continues to shadow the lives of the daughters. In response, the daughters have—perhaps unconsciously—managed to subvert their mothers' plans by ignoring their attempts to inculcate Chinese tradition into their minds and becoming so thoroughly Americanized that they retain only fragments of their cultural heritage. The result is a breakdown in communication between mothers and daughters; more like antagonists than friends, the two groups are so wary around each other that they cannot voice their frustrations and fears.

Raised by their mothers to acknowledge the existence of a system of matrilineage, Tan's Chinese mothers have a sense of generational continuity; they feel connected with their own mothers and their mothers' mothers, and they feel equally linked with their daughters. "Your mother is in your bones," says An-mei Hsu to Jing-mei Woo who admits that she knows little about her dead mother (40). Later, preparing to tell her daughter, Rose, about her own mother, An-mei muses, "I was born to my mother and I was born a girl. All of us are like stairs, one step after another, going up and down, but all going the same way" (215). Unfortunately, their American daughters do not feel the same connectedness to their heritage, and they do not recognize a symbiotic relationship between mothers and daughters; these second-generation Americans see only that their mothers appear to be trying to live through their children.

In speaking about her mother, Jing-mei Woo identifies the dream that has brought the women of her mother's generation to America, the dream that has shaped their lives and their relationships with each other and with their daughters. "My mother believed you could be anything you wanted to be in America" (132) she says, articulating a crucially important sentence that mothers and daughters interpret differently. Believing in their duty to encourage—and push, if necessary—their daughters to great heights of achievement, the mothers expect not only to be heeded but also to be allowed to share in whatever glory devolves from accomplishment; and they are baffled when their daughters, who have their own dreams, chafe at having to fulfill someone else's expectations. Because they have been schooled in the American tradition of individuality, the daughters resist their mothers' attempts to define their lives or to participate vicariously in their accomplishments. As a child embarrassed by her mother's constant bragging about her chess victories, Waverly at first asks her mother to stop announcing her name to passersby in the market. Misunderstanding the request to mean that Waverly does not wish to be seen in public with her mother, Lindo becomes very angry. Frustrated, Waverly shouts that her mother needs to learn to play chess herself so that she does not have to resort to showing off through her daughter. The rift between mother and daughter begins at that point, and continues to widen steadily through time. To Lindo Jong, pride in a daughter's talent is natural and she believes that a mother is—or should be—entitled to share in her daughter's triumphs; to Waverly, that pride represents a mother's attempt to live through her daughter, thereby denying that daughter a separate identity and a sense of personal individual achievement.

As they grow to womanhood, the daughters feel that at every turn they are reminded of their failure to live up to their mothers' expectations, and they resent what they perceive as their mothers' attempts to live through them, to mold them into the women that their mothers would like to have become. When Jing-mei tries to explain that she has learned in her psychology course that parental criticism is destructive because human beings perform well when faced with high expectations while criticism dooms individuals to inadequate achievement through the suggestion that failure is expected, Suyuan retorts that Jing-mei is too lazy even to rise to her mother's expectations. Years later, Jing-mei is still weighed down by her mother's implication that she is incapable of success.

Even as adults, the daughters live with the knowledge that they have somehow disappointed their mothers, that they have failed to live up to expectations of fame and success. During her last New Year celebration with her mother, Jing-mei finally admits to herself that she will more than likely never achieve great goals; she is perfectly competent at what she does—small projects at the advertising agency where she works—but her accomplishments are merely adequate, never spectacular. Even aggressive, successful Waverly admits that her mother makes her feel like a failure. Lunching at Waverly's favorite Chinese restaurant, Lindo criticizes Waverly's new haircut, complains about dirty chopsticks and bowls and lukewarm soup, and disputes the amount of the check. When the women stop by Waverly's apartment after lunch, Lindo denigrates a mink jacket that Rich has given Waverly, pointing out that the jacket is constructed of inferior fur. Lena St. Clair looks forward with trepidation to her mother's visit to her new home, which is an expensively converted barn, and when Ying-ying arrives, Lena's fears are justified. The older woman notices only the slanted floor, the sloping roof in the guest room, and a wobbly postmodern marble and wood table that to Ying-ying is simply a useless—and ugly—ornament.

In the daughters' imaginations, the mothers have become mythologized as potent goddesses who exhibit uncanny powers and make impossible demands on their daughters who, in turn, are powerless to resist. Rose remembers being a little girl and hearing her mother, An-mei, claim that she could see Rose and read her mind even when the child was in another room. Young Rose believed her mother because "the power of her words was that strong" (185). To Lena, her mother Ying-ying possesses an uncanny talent for seeing future events, but instead of using that ability positively, Ying-ying tends to foresee only impending disasters for the St. Clair family. Wondering if her mother "poisoned" her first marriage by being critical, Waverly fears Lindo's destructively acerbic tongue and its possible effect on her relationship with Rich. Apprehensively, she waits for Lindo to initiate a quiet, steady campaign of criticism, one word at a time, phrase by phrase, negative comment by negative comment "until his looks, his character, his soul would have eroded away" (173).

Fearful of the power that they ascribe to their mothers, the daughters respond by distancing themselves, first emotionally and then—as circumstances and finances permit them to do so—physically and geographically.

Although the Joy Luck mothers have always been aware of the gulf between themselves and their daughters, they are at a loss as to how they might bridge the distance. To the mothers, their daughters are strangers who remember nothing of their mothers' values. In a preamble to her first narrative, Lindo complains to her daughter Waverly that promises mean nothing to the younger generation. Lindo accuses Waverly of making promises to have dinner with her parents, and then cancelling dinner plans on the basis of flimsily transparent excuses: a traffic jam, a favorite movie on television, or that most invoked and most abused excuse of all time—a headache. It is clear that the daughters excuse themselves from association with the older generation by offering a familiar litany of reasons, all of which are products of contemporary Western society. Ironically, the mothers view themselves as powerless against the engulfing American culture that has estranged their daughters from the old Chinese traditions. In a kind of epiphany immediately following the Joy Luck Club dinner, Jing-mei realizes that she has been blind to the truth about her mother's friends; the aunties are old and frightened because in Jing-mei, they are forced to confront their own daughters who know nothing about the ancestral homeland or about their elders' hopes and ambitions and lost dreams. The aunties "see that joy and luck do not mean the same to their daughters, that to . . . American-born minds 'joy luck' . . . does not exist" (41). Lindo Jong, An-mei Hsu, and Ying-ying St. Clair are fearful that their generation and its dreams will be erased from the memories of their daughters, who will in turn bear children who know nothing about their Chinese heritage or the courage and resourcefulness of their emigrant forebears.

Another theme that many readers have identified in *The Joy Luck Club* is the pursuit of the American Dream, a theme with special resonance in a novel about immigrants who live in a diaspora culture. The Joy Luck mothers have all come to the United States after losing everything in China; they have traveled across an ocean to a country that has, for many Chinese, acquired mythic status as the "Gold Mountain" where immense wealth and success are possible for all who are willing to work hard. Beginning with the fable about the woman and the swan, Tan reveals the depth of the mothers' belief that in America, everyone can become rich and successful, and even immigrants can share as full partners in the bounty of the New World. Suyuan's faith in the American Dream, inspired and then nurtured by the articles she has read in American magazines like *Good Housekeeping* and *Reader's Digest*, drives her into an obsessive search for the one talent that will make her daughter famous through television and the "Ed Sullivan Show." Lindo Jong gives her children names that signal her hopes for them specifically and for the Jong family in general. She names her first son Winston because the two syllables of that name—"wins" and "ton"—suggest a sudden windfall of cash, or even fame; she calls her second son Vincent, a name with two syllables that sound to Lindo like "win" and "cent." Among the members of the Joy Luck Club, belief in the American Dream is signaled in a number of ways. For example, like their more well-heeled fellow citizens in country clubs, the club follows the activities of the stock market, and the financial report that precedes the club dinner records selling Subaru and purchasing Smith International. Less obvious is the fact that those who can afford to do so leave Chinatown and move to somewhat more upscale neighborhoods where they furnish their new homes with brand new Western-style furniture that advertises their success to their friends. The mothers achieve a small measure of success in their adopted country, but their daughters, who have fewer barriers to cross and fewer obstacles to negotiate, come closer to the promise of the American Dream.

Of the daughters, Waverly Jong best exemplifies one aspect of success according to the most familiar definition of the Dream. As a child, she enjoyed fame as a chess prodigy, winning tournaments and amassing a collection of trophies. Now a well-paid tax lawyer, Waverly enjoys the life of the upwardly mobile single mother and career woman of the

1990s. She has outgrown the local beauty shop and now gets her hair cut at an upscale establishment owned by a man who calls himself Mr. Rory. Like other successful careerists with an eye to image, she attends the symphony, takes her daughter to the zoo, and treats her mother to lunch at an expensive restaurant. Rich, her fiancé who also is an attorney, has given her a mink jacket for Christmas, and together they are planning a honeymoon in China. By any number of measures, Waverly lives the Dream—but the novel makes clear that her brand of success is not enough. Her relationship with her mother has been problematic since Waverly's childhood outburst during which she told Lindo to stop trying to live through her daughter. The distance between the two women has grown with the years; Waverly is embarrassed by her mother's stubborn adherence to Old World customs and not a little irritated by Lindo's tendency to intrude. Lindo, for her part, is aware that her daughter is ashamed of her, and that knowledge eventually leads her to begin questioning whether she did the right thing when she decided to raise her children with what she calls "American circumstances" (254).

For at least one of the mothers, the American Dream works in reverse. Ying-ying St. Clair differs from the others in several ways: she was a child of privilege and wealth, and she does not emigrate to America to have a better life. She comes as the wife of Clifford St. Clair, a man who has to court her for four years before she decides to let him marry her. Her decision comes after she learns that her first husband—her first love, from whom she is divorced—has died. For Ying-ying, marrying St. Clair is the easiest course of action, one about which she does not have to think too deeply. Despite St. Clair's belief that he has given Ying-ying the opportunity of a lifetime by taking her to the United States, Ying-ying is conscious always that in her adopted country she lives in houses smaller than those in which her family's servants lived, she does servants' work, and she wears cheap American clothes. For Ying-ying, the American Dream remains elusive and out of reach, and it remains for her daughter, Lena, to achieve a measure of success through her country home with its expensive furnishings and swimming pool.

A third theme that Amy Tan explores in the novel is relationships. The mother-daughter dyad has already been addressed previously, but other and different relationships, especially marriage, come under scrutiny as well. As a group, the mothers have not been successful in marriage. Lindo Jong is married first to a boy to whom she has been betrothed since childhood, and when that union proves to be spectacularly unsuccessful, she uses her wits creatively to devise an escape. Ying-ying St.

Clair also experiences an arranged first marriage to a man with whom she falls in love after the wedding. Her tragedy is that her husband is a womanizer who eventually leaves her for a woman with whom he has been having an affair. Ironically, if Ying-ying's first husband does not love her enough, her second loves her perhaps too well. Clifford St. Clair is so protective of his wife that he nearly obliterates her personality.

The daughters fare as badly in marriage as their mothers have done. Waverly Jong is divorced from her high school sweetheart who turned out to be irresponsible and stingy as well as inclined toward extramarital affairs. Rose Hsu and Lena St. Clair are still married, but Rose's husband has filed for divorce, and Lena's is obtusely blind to the fact that their marriage is dysfunctional beyond repair. Jing-mei Woo has never married, and does not appear likely to do so in the near future.

ALTERNATIVE READING: CULTURAL CRITICISM

Cultural Criticism

Cultural criticism is such a vast and sprawling (and growing) discipline that it is not easy to arrive at a succinct definition that will both say enough for clarity and avoid the kind of over-definition that leads inevitably to obfuscation. To understand what is being examined by the cultural critic, we need a definition of *culture*. According to Clifford Geertz, culture is a semiotic (that is, based on signs and symbols) system, a concept that he explains as follows:

> Believing with Max Weber, that man is an animal suspended in webs of significance he himself has spun, I take culture to be those webs, and the analysis of it to be therefore not an experimental science in search of a law but an interpretive one in search of meaning. (5)

In other words, culture is a human invention, a collection of hierarchies, relationships, practices, and behaviors that define the context in which an individual is expected to function as a member of a specific cultural group. Among the webs that Geertz identifies in his work are social institutions, cultural categories, patterns of socialization, habits of thinking and acting, and even modes of speaking. Race, ethnicity, class, and gender are significant cultural constructs that affect all individuals, and the points at which those constructs intersect form some of the most interesting and controversial subjects of cultural critique. Shirley Geok-Lin Lim, an Asian American literary critic, defines cultural criticism by codifying its purpose and describing its functions. She points out that cultural criticism is

> concerned with analysis of race and ethnicity, specifically the imbalance of power between dominant white groups and peoples of color and the attempt to change the unequal sets of relationships. (571)

She further suggests that cultural criticism "resists and interrogates the claim that aesthetic criteria form a dominant, autonomous, objective, privileged position," and that it views the literary text as a "lapidary of discourses from the past: memoir, myth, family and community history, folk tales, talk-story" (573). In other words, instead of relying on traditional and artificially constructed standards or criteria as guides to approaching a work of literature, the cultural critic attempts to visualize the social and cultural structures embedded in the work, and to understand the "lapidary of discourses," or narrative and artistic practices, that have shaped that work, and, in a sense, called it into being and given it a voice.

To discuss contemporary texts as well as to interrogate the cultural practices and narrative forms that underpin those texts, cultural studies embraces and synthesizes approaches from anthropology, economics, feminism and gender studies, history, literary theory, psychoanalysis, and sociology. Employing a wide-ranging vocabulary drawn from those disciplines, cultural studies has created a critical language and identified a series of crucial questions that allow for the examination of the cultural codes that are embedded in literary texts.

We begin a cultural analysis of *The Joy Luck Club* by first noting that although the work is indubitably a novel, it bears little resemblance to other novels such as—to name a few literary classics that reside securely in the canon—Jane Austen's *Pride and Prejudice*, George Eliot's *Middlemarch*, or Charlotte Brontë's *Jane Eyre*, or even such enduringly popular works of fiction as Daphne du Maurier's *Rebecca* or Margaret Mitchell's *Gone With the Wind*. Yet despite its difference from these works, *Joy Luck* has achieved the status of both classic and popular work. The contemporary text that Tan's novel most resembles is Maxine Hong Kingston's *Woman Warrior*, another hybrid multigeneric and multiperspectival text that appropriates a variety of narrative structures—many from oral traditions—and juxtaposing those structures not only with each other but also with poetry and reportage, myth and factual material, reminiscence and dream vision. Like *Joy Luck*, *Woman Warrior* appears to have earned both classic and popular labels, suggesting that these two texts have resonances for a variety of readers, both academic and nonacademic. Both Kingston and Tan employ for their novels the narrative form known as talk story (defined in Chapter 2), which allows them to privilege the voices of individuals for whom the more familiar Western narrative structures would be inappropriate and inadequate. As a narrative form, talk story provides the mothers in *The Joy Luck Club* with the structural and linguistic apparatus to tell their stories in their own words without having to resort to translation to fit the demands of the traditional Western narrative, which requires clear patterns of conflict, crisis, and denouement. Tan's text is a novel—albeit one that radically alters and expands the traditional definition of novel—that invites an examination of the ways in which Tan appropriates a variety of modes of expressive writing to accomplish her purposes: the portrayal of the immigrant experience from the distinctive point of view of first- and second-generation Americans of noticeably ethnic heritage, and the ways in which that experience radically influences the lives of some of America's ethnic minorities. Clearly, a connection exists between Tan's focus on the ethnic diaspora community and her choice of that community's multiple narrative forms to shape her text; such a choice allows the novel's characters to speak in their natural voices and customary linguistic patterns, thus giving the novel the kind of authenticity that would be lacking in a straightforward linear narrative.

The Bicultural Condition

We continue the cultural analysis of *The Joy Luck Club* by focusing on issues of identity and ethnicity or race in the novel, especially on biculturalism as a condition in which identity and race intersect, as an experience that involves existing on as well as crossing and re-crossing national, ethnic, and generational boundaries. Tan's protagonists inhabit a psychological and emotional landscape that has been labelled "the border": mothers mediate between the homeland of their birth and their adopted country; daughters feel trapped between their Chinese heritage and their American upbringing; and mothers and daughters meet uneasily in the unstable geography of the immigrant family in which one generation remains firmly entrenched in an ancestral culture while the younger family members feel like outsiders or aliens in that culture. For second-generation Americans, the dominant culture can be as unwelcoming as the ancestral culture; their black hair and brown skin ensure that these individuals cannot simply disappear into anonymity in American society. Thus they are American by birth, by education, and even by inclination, but they are marginalized by their Otherness, by their appearance that trumpets difference to the dominant culture.

In an essay entitled "Growing Up Asian in America," Kesaya Noda poses a series of crucial questions that can lead to a cultural analysis of Tan's novel. Beginning by asking how an individual might come to self-knowledge and self-definition, Noda posits two possible answers:

> From the inside—within a context that is self-defined, from a grounding in community and a connection with culture and history that are comfortably accepted? Or from the outside—in terms of messages . . . from the media and people who are often ignorant? Even as an adult I can still see two sides of my face and past. I can see from the inside out, in freedom. And . . . from the outside in, driven by the old voices of childhood and lost in anger and fear. (244)

Noda's questions suggest the existence of dual identities between which many immigrants and their children must oscillate, depending on their circumstances.

Amy Tan's Joy Luck mothers know themselves from the inside; they are secure in a Chinese cultural context that they accept. As a group, the mothers—including Ying-ying at the end of the novel—have a fairly healthy sense of their worth and a clear conception of who they are individually. Proudly displaying her gold bracelets, Lindo Jong says that to the Chinese, fourteen-carat gold has very little worth, and she notes that her own jewelry is made of twenty-four-carat gold. Later, she explains that she buys only the most expensive gold bracelets to commemorate her escape from a bad marriage because she feels that she is worth the luxury. Ying-ying at first seems disconnected and lost, but her daughter's distress goads her into confronting the memory of her failed first marriage and the child that she aborted, the source of the emotional pain that led to her depression. Having voiced her loss, Ying-ying is able to remember that she was born in the Year of the Tiger (a reference to the traditional Chinese designation for the year of her birth), and with that recollection she gains the strength to reclaim her "tiger spirit," so that she can pass it on to her daughter. The mothers' self-knowledge and centeredness come from their "grounding in community and a connection with culture and history" (Noda 244). Deep in their hearts, they have carried from their ancestral culture what Orville Schell describes as a "sustaining fund of memory" (3), the heritage that they are trying to pass on to their daughters.

It is the mothers who talk story to give shape and significance to their lives. Their distinctive linguistic patterns and images fit comfortably with the conventions of popular narrative and oral tradition; moreover, their experiences defy description through conventional narrative structures. Wendy Ho points out that *The Joy Luck Club* foregrounds the stories of women whose lives have been neglected, women who feel the need to transmit their stories to their daughters who need to know their mothers' lives if they are to integrate comfortably the two cultures into which they have been born:

> The personal stories of the Joy Luck mothers do battle through gossip, circular talking, cryptic messages/caveats, dream images, bilingual language, and talk-story traditions—not in the linear, logical, or publicly authorized discourse in patriarchal or imperialist narratives. (339)

Talk story empowers the mothers, something that the dominant culture has failed to do for the daughters who remain mired in uncertainty about their identities, about their place in the culture that they want to claim as theirs.

The Joy Luck daughters have not experienced the cultural connectedness that sustains their mothers. Caught between the Chinese and American cultures, unable to connect with their mothers' memories of a homeland that they have never seen, and unable because of their visible ethnicity to blend effortlessly into the American melting pot, the daughters derive the shapes and outlines of their identities from the images and icons of popular culture, as well as from media-generated images of success and fulfillment. Waverly Jong exemplifies the instability of identity that has plagued the daughters. When Lindo tells Waverly that the way she carries herself will mark her instantly as an outsider and as an American when she goes to China, Waverly is displeased. At Waverly's "sour American look," Lindo ruminates that although Waverly now wants to be labelled Chinese because ethnicity has become fashionable, her interest has awakened nearly too late, and she remembers almost nothing of what Lindo tried to teach her years earlier. Lindo notes that Waverly as a child paid lip service to the role of the traditional Chinese daughter, listening to Lindo's stories about China and paying some attention to the lessons embedded in those stories. But Waverly performs according to Lindo's "Chinese ways" only while she is still dependent on her mother, "only until she learned how to walk out the door." Now, Waverly is almost totally assimilated, Chinese in skin and hair color but thoroughly "American-made" in her values, her language, and her identity (254). Significantly, the daughter through whose story the others' narratives are mediated discards her American name, June, in favor of her Chinese name, Jing-mei. As Jing-mei, she journeys to her mother's ancestral homeland, China, and completes the circle of her heritage by claiming her Chinese half-sisters. But even as Jing-mei travels to her ancestral homeland, she still is a Chinese American—a stranger who is visiting a country that is foreign to her.

The Chinese American Experience

For many Chinese Americans, life in the United States is a series of dualities—two identities, two voices, two cultures, and even two names—that represent an uneasy stance somewhere between the traditional Chinese culture of their own or their parents' homeland and the contemporary American culture in which they have chosen to live or into which they have been born. Maxine Hong Kingston articulates the position poetically in *Woman Warrior*:

> Chinese-Americans, when you try to understand what things in you are Chinese, how do you separate what is peculiar to childhood, to poverty, insanities, one family, your mother who marked your growing with stories, from what is Chinese? What is Chinese tradition and what is the movies? (5–6)

Kingston eventually comes to the conclusion that the Chinese American identity cannot be divided simply into two ethnic halves, independent of each other, each retaining the distinctive characteristics of its origins, and she refuses to portray her identity as unified.

Orville Schell observes that after China opened its borders to travelers from the West in the 1970s, older Chinese emigrants who cherished memories of life before Mao Zedong welcomed the chance to revisit the homeland from which they had been exiled since 1949. Their children, however, "looked with deep ambivalence on the idea of having to awaken a dormant Chinese side in themselves" (3). It is this ambivalence that paralyzes Jing-mei when her Joy Luck aunties suggest that she travel to China; the same cultural uneasiness prompts Waverly to worry that she will look so much like the native Chinese that U.S. Immigration officials will bar her from re-entering the United States at the end of her trip.

Only tenuously connected with the ancestral home about which their mothers speak frequently, the daughters in *The Joy Luck Club* are more conscious of the complexities of living as hyphenated Americans in a society that privileges homogeneity. Heirs to a range of opportunities that their mothers never had, the daughters must nevertheless deal with American society's inability to define them without stereotyping. More than their mothers, they are aware that they are neither Chinese nor American, that they are American by birth and education, but they are Chinese because their features force comparisons with white Americans. In need of some form of cultural identity, the daughters direct their best efforts toward unconditional assimilation and acculturation. They want to belong. Rose defiantly labels herself an American when her mother objects to her dating Ted Jordan on the grounds that he is an American (117). Unhappy as a child with her Asian eyes, Lena tried to make her eyes look rounder by pushing their outer corners in toward the center of her face. The daughters manage to succeed somewhat in blending into the mainstream: they refuse to learn to speak Chinese; unlike thousands of other Asian Americans they are not physicians or engineers (they are a restaurant designer who majored in Asian American studies in college, an advertising copywriter who is a college dropout, a tax lawyer, and a graphics production assistant); they marry men whom their mothers consider to be foreigners because they are not Chinese. But the price that the daughters pay for their assimilation is their nagging sense of unease in the identities that they have laboriously created for themselves. Worse yet, as Wendy Ho notes, another cost of assimilation is "the miscommunications between the Joy Luck mothers and daughters" (338). Without a language in which both the mothers and their daughters are fluent, the mothers cannot share the stories and the wisdom that can help their daughters to feel comfortable in their cultural contexts.

A particularly painful facet of the Chinese American experience is racism. The media label of "model minority" notwithstanding, Chinese Americans, along with other Americans of Asian origin, must frequently confront discrimination and prejudice, or, at the very least, stereotyping that is an insidious form of racism. In *The Joy Luck Club*, Amy Tan illustrates one form of racism through Rose Hsu's encounter with her future mother-in-law, Mrs. Jordan, who carefully explains why Rose must not marry Ted. Assuring Rose that the Jordans—unlike other unnamed people—are open-minded and harbor no prejudice against minorities, Mrs. Jordan further confides that she and Mr. Jordan "personally [know] many fine people who [are] Oriental." She reveals also that their circle of acquaintances includes even individuals of Hispanic or African-American ancestry. Reminding Rose that Ted wants to be a physician and that physicians and their wives have to conform to certain social expectations, Mrs. Jordan remarks that "it [is] so unfortunate . . . how unpopular the Vietnam War [is]" (118). Thus she implies that by continuing the relationship with Ted, Rose would certainly jeopardize his chances for a successful medical career. When Mrs. Jordan points out that she is "personally" acquainted with many "fine" minority individuals, she inadvertently reveals a bigotry that is so ingrained in her that she is unaware of its existence. She further displays her insensitivity by suggesting through her reference to the Vietnam War that all Asians are interchangeable—a common misperception and one that disturbs most Americans of Asian origin.

We do need to note that prejudice is not the exclusive property of the dominant culture; in her own fashion, Rose's mother is no less bigoted than Mrs. Jordan. On meeting Ted Jordan for the first time, An-mei Hsu cautions Rose against the relationship, voicing her disapproval of the young man by identifying him as a *waigoren*, a foreigner, thus relegating Ted to marginal status in her own—and, she hopes, her daughter's—Chinatown culture. Like Mrs. Jordan, An-mei Hsu fears that she might lose her child, and by extension her grandchildren, to someone from an alien culture.

The Chinese American experience is characterized by deep divisions, disjunctions, contrasts, and seemingly irreconcilable oppositions, not just between individuals or groups of individuals but also within personal identities. Being Chinese American is not the "happy marriage of East and West" of Broadway musical or popular fiction fame, nor is it simply a matter of choosing to be either more Asian or more Western. Being Chinese American means living with duality and division, with contrast and opposition. And those divisions and dualities become very real and very personal for Lindo Jong as she sits in Mr. Rory's beauty parlor, listening to her daughter, Waverly, and Mr. Rory discuss her as if she is not present. Lindo is acutely aware that she is in the hairdresser's chair because her daughter is ashamed of her mother and worried about what her American husband's parents will think of "this backward old Chinese woman" (255), and she fumes in silence when Waverly repeats to her in an artificially loud voice what Mr. Rory is saying, as though Lindo does not understand English. But Lindo is accustomed to this treatment and she simply smiles:

> I use my American face. . . . the face Americans think is Chinese, the one they cannot understand. But inside . . . I am ashamed . . . [b]ecause she is my daughter and I am proud of her, and I am her mother but she is not proud of me. (255)

Lindo also has a "Chinese face" that she dons smugly when Mr. Rory comments, to Waverly's initial displeasure, that the two women are uncannily similar. Lindo's awareness of her two faces reveals that she is conscious of her dual identity in ways that Waverly cannot begin to understand. Waverly has assimilated so thoroughly and has so internalized her Western identity that she is guilty of treating her mother like a non-English–speaking alien—in effect, Waverly has positioned herself on the other side of a cultural divide from her mother.

For Lindo, Waverly's position is both triumph and defeat. Lindo has wanted her children to have what she calls "American circumstances" in addition to their "Chinese character," and Waverly has certainly achieved American-style success: she is a tax lawyer, she has a daughter whom she loves, and she is about to marry another tax lawyer. In addition, her English is fluent and idiomatic, and her close friends are not Chinese but rather other young white professionals. As Lindo points out, "Only her skin and hair are Chinese. Inside—she is all American made" (254). To Lindo's great disappointment, she has been unsuccessful at instructing Waverly in what "Chinese character" entails: the ability to keep one's thoughts hidden to gain every advantage in every situation; the acceptance of the fact that easy goals are never worth pursuing; and the continuing acknowledgment of self-worth.

Ultimately, Lindo Jong is left with only questions that even she cannot answer, questions about the choices she has made, questions that deepen the divisions in her soul. She has come to America with high ambitions, with the intention of giving her children the best opportunities available, but in her old age, she begins to wonder whether she has made the right decisions:

> I think about my intentions. Which one is American? Which one is Chinese? Which one is better? If you show one, you must always sacrifice the other. . . . So now I think, What did I lose? What did I get back in return? (266)

Lindo recalls her return to China after a long absence of decades. On that trip, she had been careful not to flaunt fancy jewelry or wear loud colors—the marks of a tourist; she spoke Chinese fluently and handled local currency with ease; she did everything in her power to blend in with the local residents. Nevertheless, Lindo was treated like a wealthy visitor who could afford artificially inflated prices. Clearly, something ineffable about her—her appearance, her carriage, her manner—had changed. Remembering that experience, Lindo not only realizes that she is no longer truly Chinese, but also that in the eyes of people like Mr. Rory and her own daughter, she is not American. She is Chinese American; she inhabits a space on the border between two worlds, belonging to neither world completely, destined to live permanently in that border country.

4

The Kitchen God's Wife
(1991)

In 1991, two years after her tremendous success with *The Joy Luck Club*, Amy Tan published *The Kitchen God's Wife*. Like many writers whose first books have received spectacular and widespread attention, Tan admits that she was more than a little apprehensive about the critical and popular reception that her second published novel would receive, knowing that reviewers and readers would inevitably be unable to resist comparing the second book with the first. In fact, she points out in "Angst and the Second Novel," she agonized so much about her second novel that she damaged her health and suffered from debilitating physical discomfort:

> I developed literal symptoms of the imagined weight of my task . . . a pain in my neck, which later radiated to my jaw, resulting in constant gnashing, then two cracked teeth and, finally a huge dental bill. The pain then migrated down my back. (5)

Amy Tan did ultimately complete a novel for publication, but only after she had "deleted hundreds of pages from [her] computer's memory" (7). In fact, she estimates that "the outtakes must now number close to a thousand pages" (6).

Interestingly, *The Kitchen God's Wife* was not actually Amy Tan's sec-

ond novel; it was, instead, only one of Tan's numerous attempts to produce another novel after *The Joy Luck Club* was published. Tan describes
the plots of several pieces of fiction that she never completed:

> 88 pages . . . about the daughter of a scholar, who accidentally
> kills a magistrate. . . . 56 pages . . . about a Chinese girl or-
> phaned during the San Francisco earthquake of 1906. . . . 95
> pages about a young girl . . . in northeast China during the
> 1930s with her missionary parents. . . . 30 pages about a
> woman disguised as a man who becomes a sidewalk scribe to
> the illiterate workers of Chinatown. ("Angst" 6)

In all, Amy Tan started—and abandoned—seven potential novels before she completed the eighth "lucky" attempt, which became her highly
acclaimed second published novel.

Like Tan's first novel, *The Kitchen God's Wife* addresses the relationship—and the conflicts—between a Chinese immigrant mother (Winnie)
and her American-born daughter (Pearl). But the true focus of the novel
is less on the mother-daughter dyad and more predominantly on the
story of a woman who is born into wealth and position in pre-communist
China, endures a degrading arranged marriage and the early deaths of
three children, lives through World War II, emigrates to America, and
successfully creates a relatively comfortable and stable life for herself in
a new country and an alien culture.

The novel opens with Pearl Louie Brandt, a second-generation Chinese
American who seems to have all but repudiated her Chinese heritage
while embracing her American identity. Dreading her mother's reaction,
Pearl has concealed for seven years the fact that she is afflicted with
multiple sclerosis. Her reticence is not born solely out of a desire to
protect her mother from an unpleasant shock, but also from the fact that
Pearl has deliberately excluded her mother from many arenas of her life.
In fact, Pearl rarely visits her mother, whose bossy criticisms and pervasive superstitions have created an emotional and cultural gulf between the two women. When family loyalties and responsibilities obligate
Pearl to return to her childhood home to attend a cousin's engagement
party and the funeral of an elderly aunt, she is forced by the circumstances and her proximity to her mother, as well as by her Auntie Helen's
persistent and unsubtle prodding, to confront the reasons for her
uncomfortable relationship with her mother. Winnie, in her turn, takes

advantage of Pearl's homecoming to reveal to her daughter her own terrible secrets.

Winnie Louie's narrative—the life story that she has so carefully withheld from her entire family for decades—is the heart and sinew of *The Kitchen God's Wife*. The tale is riveting, both for the astonishing events of Winnie's life and for the quietly understated way in which she reveals, episode by painful episode, the saga of her psychological journey from being Weili, the young hopeful woman who had dreams of fulfilling her role as a good wife, to becoming Winnie, the brave and indomitable woman who flees China and a deranged ex-husband a scant five days before the communist takeover closed the Chinese border. Along that epic journey from one self to another, Winnie experiences abuse inflicted by a sadistic husband, grief over the deaths of her babies, the brutality of the Japanese war with China, hunger, poverty, homelessness, and the horrors of a countryside ravaged by bombs and fighting. When family events bring Winnie's daughter, Pearl, home to Chinatown, Winnie finally is presented with the opportunity to tell the story that she has protected for decades, and as Pearl listens to and truly hears her mother's stories, she arrives at an understanding of why and how Winnie has become the woman she is. Slowly and carefully, mother and daughter begin to build a friendship, a relationship forged in truth and open communication. At the end of the novel, when all secrets have been revealed, Winnie presents Pearl with a statue of the Kitchen God's wife, a woman who has no official place in the traditional Chinese pantheon of gods and goddesses, but who has nonetheless quietly, patiently endured so much abuse from her husband and weathered her trials with such grace and dignity that Winnie's deification of her is as perfectly appropriate as is Winnie's gift of the Kitchen God's Wife to Pearl.

PLOT DEVELOPMENT

The Kitchen God's Wife involves two plots: a frame story set in the United States and involving primarily Pearl and her mother Winnie, and a central, focal narrative about Winnie's life as Jiang Weili in China before World War II, during the war, and immediately before her emigration to the United States to become Winnie Louie.

The opening sentence of *The Kitchen God's Wife* immediately places the reader in the middle of what appears to be an ongoing debate, as Pearl announces that each time she and her mother have a conversation, Winnie begins "as if we were already in the middle of an argument" (11). Although there is no clearly identifiable conflict between mother and daughter, their relationship is strained, uneasy, characterized by a rift that slowly is widening in a process that neither woman seems able to halt. The novel's first two chapters, which are narrated by Pearl to an unidentified general audience, introduce the framing plot within which the major narrative is developed. In those early chapters, Pearl details her irritation with her mother's actions, her frustration with herself for allowing her mother to affect her so negatively, and finally the sudden release of her long-suppressed grief for her father who died a quarter of a century earlier. Pearl also introduces—in addition to herself and her mother—Helen Kwong whose own story intersects with Winnie's story, and whose decision to reveal long-hidden truths precipitates both Winnie's epic confession and Pearl's revelations.

Winnie narrates the next two chapters to herself, as she slowly tries to make sense of sudden new developments in her eventful life. Helen has shared with her a recent letter from a mutual friend in China, announcing that Winnie's first husband, Wen Fu, has just died. To Helen, the news means one thing—she and Winnie are now free to stop living their shared lie; they can tell the true story of the early years of their friendship. To Winnie, the letter is a jolting and extremely unwelcome reminder of a past that she has kept buried for forty years or more; and Helen's reaction forces Winnie to make a decision: Pearl must hear the story from her mother and not from Helen. Having made up her mind to tell her daughter about the China years, Winnie telephones Pearl and asks her to come for a visit immediately.

Save for one chapter, Winnie shapes and dominates the rest of the novel with her voice as she recounts to Pearl, episode by episode, celebration after celebration, heartbreak following heartbreak, the story of Jiang Weili. Winnie's stories are punctuated by brief reminiscences about Pearl's difficult adolescence, by remarks about Helen, by introspective philosophizing, by rhetorical questions. Again and again, Winnie interrupts her storytelling with homely comments—about the need to go into the kitchen to make more tea, about how she no longer likes to eat celery, about a burned out light bulb—and each remark contributes to the sense that Winnie is sharing these stories with her daughter as they sit companionably sipping tea or move from room to room in Winnie's home. The juxtaposition of a domestic American scene with the horrific events in the China stories serves to emphasize Winnie's resilience and to highlight the distance and magnitude of her physical, psychological, and emotional journeys.

Pearl speaks only one more time, just before the end of the novel, and right after Winnie's calm revelation that Wen Fu is Pearl's father. For Pearl, the news is an unpleasant surprise, but she quickly overcomes her initial shock with the realization of what it must have cost Winnie to re-live through storytelling a traumatic past that has lain buried in Winnie's memory since before Pearl's birth. Admiration for Winnie invests Pearl with the courage to tell her mother about her own illness. Pearl's con-fession immediately gives Winnie something on which to focus in the present. Having divested herself of the baggage of a terrible past, Winnie is now ready to put all of her maternal energies into discovering a way to alleviate her daughter's distress.

In an epilogue, Winnie and Helen go to a Chinatown shop that spe-cializes in statues of the principal Chinese deities. As her first significant act in her campaign to help Pearl in the fight against the debilitating effects of multiple sclerosis, Winnie is searching for the perfect goddess to install on the traditional altar that Great Auntie Du has left to Pearl. In the final scene between mother and daughter, Winnie proudly pre-sents a new goddess—the Kitchen God's Wife renamed Lady Sorrowfree, canonized by Winnie to become the divine protector of all women who must endure pain and loneliness.

POINT OF VIEW AND STRUCTURE

Amy Tan allows the main characters in *The Kitchen God's Wife* to speak in their own voices, to recount the significant events of their lives as they each remember them, and to structure their life stories according to the requirements of their personal situations and their reasons for narrating the stories. Each woman constructs her own life script as she has un-derstood it, laying bare to scrutiny and criticism the choices she has made and describing without flinching the consequences of those choices. Thus, the novel is fictional autobiography, a woman's narrative of her life and experiences. Significantly, Amy Tan has said on a number of occasions that *The Kitchen God's Wife* is her mother's story, and indeed, the outlines of the novel and many of the specific details in the text are congruent with the story of Daisy Tan's life.

Although Pearl speaks first, the major voice in the novel is that of Winnie Louie, a strong and opinionated woman who greatly resembles the mothers of *The Joy Luck Club*. Like those women, Winnie has lived through the last years of feudal China as well as through the devastation of World War II, and like them she has come to the United States to begin again and to build a new, comfortable life for herself. For decades, her emotional and psychological strength enables her to suppress the story of her past and maintain silence about her terrible fears, but encroaching age and infirmity have combined to create in her the urgent need to tell her story to her only daughter.

Winnie has had a good life with Jimmy Louie in America; she has found a measure of peace and well-being in her adopted country, and she has raised a daughter who is a successful professional. But Winnie's interior life continues to be disfigured by the secret that she has guarded for over thirty years, and she is growing increasingly conscious that she has little time left in which to set the record straight. For Winnie, the act of storytelling affords a strategy for mediating her past. Breaking her silence, she pieces together into a personal epic the narrative fragments of her hidden past by speaking aloud the milestones of that long-ago existence, and by describing the events that marked her painful passage from toddler to young girl and adolescent to adult woman. Winnie's voice is that of the survivor, but it also is the voice of a mother who is compelled to share the story of her life with her daughter to give that daughter the strength she needs to confront the problems that threaten to overwhelm her existence.

Ample evidence exists to show that Pearl is the audience for whom and to whom Winnie tells her stories, hoping that somehow Pearl will hear, will understand, and will finally absolve her mother of the emotional crime of concealing the truth. Winnie has concealed a great deal. As a preamble to her life story, she apologizes for not having shared with Pearl the story of her own mother—Pearl's grandmother—and how she abandoned six-year-old Weili. Admitting at last her reluctance to believe that her mother could and did leave her, Winnie launches into her personal history, forcing herself to begin with her memories of the beautiful mother who disappeared from her life so early. Winnie's asides indicate that she is at least subliminally aware that Pearl finds her mother embarrassing at times, incomprehensible at others. Immediately after admitting that she was slow to realize that war had come to China, she speculates that Pearl more than likely thinks that her mother must be slow-witted. But Winnie perseveres with her mission. Later, when she confesses that she had an abortion after every pregnancy resulting from rape by her husband, Winnie pleads with Pearl to understand that she did not want to lose those babies, but she could not bear the children of a brute who was simply using her body to satisfy his insatiable sexual urges. Instinctively, Winnie knew that with Wen Fu as a father, a baby's life would be impossible and painful. Finally, when she re-lives her last dreadful day in China by telling the story of how her former husband raped her for the penultimate time, Winnie concludes her narrative simply by saying that she has never before told anyone—not even her beloved Jimmy—about that final dreadful violation that so nearly destroyed her soul and her will to live. And at that point, she drops her bombshell: nine months after the rape, she gave birth to Pearl in America.

In the second chapter of the novel, Pearl describes how Winnie tells Tessa and Cleo, Pearl's daughters, the traditional Chinese folktale about how the rich farmer, Zhang, becomes the Kitchen God. According to Winnie's tale, Zhang squanders all of his considerable wealth on a passionate affair with pretty Lady Li. He forces his wife to cook for his paramour, and when Lady Li chases his wife out of the house, he does not protest or intercede for his wronged wife. When Zhang's money is gone, Lady Li abandons him. Reduced to beggary, Zhang is taken in by a charitable woman who is—he realizes in horror—his discarded wife! Ashamed of his earlier treatment of his wife, Zhang tries to avoid a confrontation by jumping into the fireplace. He burns to death and his ashes float up the chimney to heaven. In heaven, the Jade Emperor decides that Zhang, who has shown the capacity for shame, should be rewarded with deification. Zhang becomes the Kitchen God, responsible for judging the behavior of mortals each year. During each New Year celebration period, the Kitchen God reports to the Emperor the names of those who should be rewarded with good luck for their exemplary lives, as well as the names of those who deserve bad luck as punishment for having behaved irresponsibly or badly. This folktale provides Amy Tan with the basic narrative outline for her novel by introducing the trope of the abused wife. *The Kitchen God's Wife* is a retelling of the Kitchen God's story—from a contemporary feminist point of view. In the traditional version of the tale, the wife disappears from the narrative after her husband has been elevated to the divine pantheon; but in Tan's version, Weili, the wife who endures her husband's abuse and philandering, is rewarded for her forbearance with another chance to experience happiness, and she becomes Winnie, the survivor, the beloved wife of a good man, the mother of an accomplished daughter, and the grandmother of two American children.

SETTING

In *The Kitchen God's Wife*, Amy Tan re-creates the intricately textured world of the Chinese American community, a world that encompasses San Francisco's alive and bustling Chinatown neighborhoods as well as the China of over half a century earlier, a homeland that exists only in the memories and stories of the older generation. Tan's settings, richly embellished with cultural and geographical detail, provide the backdrops for the drama of Winnie's life in China and her subsequent escape to America, as well as for the conflict between Pearl and Winnie, and for the cultural and generational differences that underlie the strained relations between mother and daughter.

Pearl inhabits a landscape that straddles, somewhat uncomfortably, the disparate geographies of Chinatown and mainstream California. The Chinatown of her childhood, also the Chinatown in which her mother still lives, is a place bustling with commerce and activity, with Chinese residents going about their daily business and tourists gawking at what they consider to be "exotic" sights. Among those sights are various Chinese trade associations and family societies, including a business that specialize in sending ancestor memorials to China; a fortune teller; the Sam Fook Trading Company, purveyor of good luck charms, statues of deities guaranteed to bring good luck, and a variety of objects and artifacts essential to traditional Buddhist funerals—spirit money, paper jewelry, and other similar merchandise; the First Chinese Baptist Church; and the Ding Ho Flower Shop, owned and operated by Winnie Louie and her friend Helen. Tourists are not the only Western intrusions into the determinedly Asian streets and neighborhoods. Some of Chinatown's long-time residents are noticeably Westernized: first-generation immigrants furnish their flats with nubby tweed sofas and videotape their family funerals, while their second-generation American children affect colorful spiky punk hairdos and flaunt their nose rings.

Winnie's narrative brings to life an exotic, alien China of the 1920s and the 1930s in all of its feudal glory and beauty, and then describes in horrifying detail the brutal tenor of existence in occupied China of World War II. The contrast between the two Chinas focuses attention on and underscores the changes that Weili must undergo as the enclosed worlds of her childhood and adolescence disintegrate around her, giving way to a frightening new China that she does not recognize—the China that she ultimately flees.

Shanghai, the city of Winnie's early years, is a colorful and wealthy metropolis, reveling in its ties to European culture and its roots in feudal China, basking in its cosmopolitanism and tradition, and caught between the old and the new, between East and West. Home to some of China's wealthiest businessmen as well as a sizeable European and American community, Shanghai of the 1920s and 1930s is somewhat schizophrenic in its attempts to identify itself to the world as both a traditional Chinese city and a modern Western metropolis. Winnie remembers that her mother took her to the most exclusive Western shops, purveyors of the best that the international community had to offer—from French leather shoes to that quintessentially American treat, the ice cream sundae. They go to the theatre to watch American movies featuring Charlie Chaplin and Fatty Arbuckle. Winnie describes afternoons of sitting in a theatre and watching policemen and cowboys, fire trucks and horses on the screen. Despite the pervasive European and American influences, Shanghai is indelibly Chinese. Winnie tells of watching a man "spitting a long stream of bean curd paste into a pot of boiling water"(94), and later noticing that the bean curd paste had metamorphosed into thin noodles. Away from Shanghai, in other cities, in rural areas, and on the island to which Weili goes to live with her uncle's family, China is still a richly textured ancient culture of festivals and celebrations, matchmakers and go-betweens, and feudal social hierarchies.

Marriage immediately before the outbreak of World War II catapults Weili into unfamiliar and frightening territory, and into a world of deprivation and chaos. And although she is no stranger to pain, her only real prior experience is with the hurtful indifference with which her uncle's family has treated her, and with the ensuing loneliness that marred her adolescent years. Her new life introduces her to pain in all of its manifestations—physical, emotional, spiritual, and psychological.

For Weili, wartime China is a crowded jumble of temporary housing—mud huts with crumbling walls, planks of wood in a pig shed, an old hotel—and food shortages. Roads are choked with military traffic and with people who have been evacuated from demolished towns and cities. Epidemics of cholera and other contagious diseases ravage the population, and as the war continues, bombing raids become an almost daily occurrence. Chaos in the country is reflected not only in Wen Fu's disordered mind but also in his hurtling descent into the world of the psychopath, and Weili almost immediately discovers that she has married a monster. As China disintegrates under the Japanese assault, Wen Fu slides into pure brutishness, and the end of the war does nothing to halt his plunge toward evil.

Weili's salvation comes in the form of an American soldier of Chinese ancestry, a man she meets at an American dance that is held to celebrate a Chinese American victory. The venue for the dance, a paper-bedecked warehouse, is festooned with unfamiliar homemade paper decorations and boasts an object that is completely foreign to Weili, a Christmas tree decked with red ribbons, Christmas cards, strings of popcorn, and cotton balls that are supposed to represent snow. Dozens of young Chinese dance to American music and nibble on the popcorn; they feast on brownies and cheese, and they practice speaking English, trying to twist their tongues around strange sounding words and peculiar sound combinations. For Weili, the setting is almost bizarre, so radically different from anything she has known that she feels out of place in the midst of the alien revelry. But although she does not realize its significance until much later, this foreign dance is the one bright moment in her wartime life; before the evening is over, she meets Jimmy Louie who will be her future.

Caught not only between tradition and innovation but also between East and West, the China of Weili's early life foreshadows the Chinatown in which Weili—renamed Winnie—raises her daughter, Pearl. As a young girl and later as a young married woman, Weili lives in a culture that has been infiltrated with European and American influences, all of which are eagerly adopted by young people despite the best efforts of their elders to maintain the traditional Chinese way of life. Although as a child, Weili does acquire Western tastes from her young mother, she is transformed into a traditional Chinese woman by the aunt who completes her rearing. Ironically, Pearl—like her second-generation peers in Chinatown—is thoroughly Americanized and very much determined to shed all vestige of a way of life that she and they associate with their old-fashioned and hopelessly unassimilated elders.

Tan's settings, both past and present, parallel and mirror each other, serving as bridges between Winnie and Pearl, as well as between China and America. Thus, pre-communist Shanghai with its multiple identities and cultural confusions serves to foreshadow the dilemma in which Pearl finds herself, uncomfortably positioned between her Chinese heritage and the idea of an ancestral home—personified in the mother who so ably and unconsciously irritates her—and a thoroughly American way of life that includes a husband, two daughters, a university degree, and a career.

CHARACTER DEVELOPMENT

Amy Tan has created characters who embody in a number of ways the cultural dislocations that are so much a part of the novel's settings. The collision of East and West is evident even in characters who appear only briefly: Winnie's mother finds it difficult to decide whether to wear a Chinese dress or a Western dress; some years later, during a traditional New Year celebration, Winnie's cousin Peanut sallies forth robed in an inappropriate but expensive Western coat, with her face heavily made up to resemble a movie star whom Peanut has admired in a foreign beauty magazine. Through their contact with American servicemen during the war, the younger Chinese delightedly acquire English names: a pilot named Jiaguo becomes "Jock" and dozens of giggling girls become "Donna, Dotty, Patty, Peggy, Sally, Susie, Maggie, Mattie, Jeannie, Judy" (305). In the major characters of the novel, however, cultural dissonances and tensions are deeper and more pervasive, and thus more subtly outlined.

Although her story opens the novel, Pearl Louie Brandt is not a particularly interesting woman, and it is quite possible that Amy Tan has deliberately created a less than memorable character to focus major attention on Winnie Louie. Pearl is forty years old, married to a physician named Phil, and reasonably successful in her career as a speech and language clinician. She also is the mother of two daughters, confident Tessa and gentle Cleo. On the surface, Pearl appears to be living the American Dream, but very early in her narrative, her dissatisfaction with life becomes evident. The cause of her discontent, she reveals obliquely, is her problematic relationship with her mother.

About her difficult relationship with Winnie, Pearl remarks that whenever she is forced to spend time in her mother's company, she feels as though she must constantly be on her guard, "avoiding land mines" (16). Pearl admits that she and Phil have quarreled about her reactions to her mother's remarks and assumptions, and it is clear that whatever Winnie's intent might have been at any given time, Pearl has allowed Winnie's opinions to color her own worldview. On hearing that Pearl has been offered a job over two other candidates, Winnie does not congratulate her daughter, but asks instead why only two other people were interested in the position. Winnie's caustic criticism exacerbates Pearl's nagging worry that although she is happy in the position, she might have missed a better and more desirable opportunity. Sadly, Pearl's slight discomfort with the way her life has turned out colors her narrative—her voice is somewhat querulous, tinged with complaint and not a little regret at missing something she cannot identify.

Several times, Pearl has planned to tell Winnie about the multiple sclerosis that is very slowly eroding Pearl's physical health, but each time the younger woman begins to broach the subject, her mother interrupts with a long monologue precipitated by one word or phrase in Pearl's tentative introduction of her news; each time, Pearl allows her mother's interruption to stem the flow of her confession. And with each foiled attempt to inform her mother, Pearl grows more frustrated and more apprehensive that somehow Winnie will find out from someone else. Perhaps because Pearl's narration seems to be a long litany of irritations and only partial successes, the novel gets off to a slow start, and does not truly begin to engage the reader until Winnie begins to speak her piece.

Winnie Louie is the dominant character of the novel and its most voluble storyteller, but it is as Jiang Weili that she is tried in the crucible of tradition and experience. Born the daughter of an aristocratic and quite elderly Shanghai businessman and his replacement second wife, Weili spends her childhood as the pampered daughter of a wealthy man who houses his wives in a large, elaborately designed, and ornately furnished dwelling. Although traditional enough to permit himself the luxury of multiple wives, Weili's father has embraced Western culture sufficiently to provide his second wife—Weili's mother—with the English biscuits, French gloves and shoes, Hamilton watches, White Russian soap, and Italian cars that she passionately adores.

Weili is only six years old when her mother abruptly and mysteriously disappears from her life. Although Weili manages to piece together from overheard conversations and politely euphemistic explanations a few fragments of information about her mother's fate, she never fully understands what has become of the mother who spoiled her during those very early years. Weili is sent by her father to live with an uncle and his family, and while they do not mistreat her, they ignore her, making it clear that she is unimportant and unworthy of their affection. Her lonely childhood helps her to hone the skill of silent endurance, a characteristic that will later enable her to conceal her secrets for decades.

At eighteen, Weili marries Wen Fu, a handsome young man who has been described by the matchmaker who approaches her family as the scion of a wealthy clan that runs a thriving import business. Years later, in telling the story of the marriage to Pearl, Winnie remembers that she was happy about the wedding, but not in the way that a new bride would be. She admits that she did not love her new husband even at the beginning of the marriage, but that despite the absence of romance or even friendship in the match, she was happy because marriage for her represented a chance to have a life that was better than her comfortable but emotionally sterile existence at her uncle's house. In retrospect, she wonders whether she might not also have confused her happiness with love.

That new opportunity for a different kind of life turns out to be the worst fate that could happen to Weili. Not only has her new husband lied about the extent of his family's assets, but he has also misrepresented himself. His charming manners are a facade—he is a monster at heart. Trapped in a degrading marriage for several years while a war rages around her, Weili endures humiliation, abuse, and even rape at the hands of her husband. She bears three children, all of whom die in infancy or babyhood. Her capacity for stoicism stands her in good stead, and she discovers in herself additional capabilities, including a strong will to live and an urge to fight for her future.

Two characters figure prominently in Winnie's narrative, and they deserve some scrutiny in the context of their impact on Weili's life. Wen Fu, the man whom Weili marries at eighteen, embodies the fate that shapes her into a survivor; and Hulan, Weili's oldest friend, represents the continuity of life and the connection between past and present.

After he marries Weili, Wen Fu develops into such a villainous creature that he is a nearly one-dimensional monster. A number of readers and critics have, in fact, noted that Amy Tan has not populated her fictional world with well-rounded, completely believable male characters. When Weili first meets Wen Fu, he is charming and likeable, and apparently interested in her cousin Peanut, who, in turn, is so intrigued with the handsome young man that she begins meeting him in secret and sending him love notes. On discovering that Weili's father is far wealthier and more socially prominent than Peanut's family, Wen Fu immediately drops his clandestine courtship of Peanut and persuades his family to hire a go-between to propose a marriage between him and Weili—and Weili, who is totally unaware of the reason for the proposal but somewhat puzzled by Wen Fu's sudden interest in her, becomes his wife.

Not long after the wedding, Wen Fu's concealed psychosis surfaces, and Weili abruptly awakens from her dream of a happy life to the reality of marriage to a dishonest, sadistic bully. Meanwhile, enamored of the glamorous aura surrounding the very few Chinese men who have been trained as pilots, and desirous of joining that elite fraternity, Wen Fu appropriates the educational documents and identity papers belonging to his dead brother—a much more accomplished and capable man—and manages to gain admission, under his brother's name, to a flight training program. Somehow, he manages to earn his pilot's wings. He then contrives to spend the war years discovering strategies for evading air combat; thus he survives the war more or less unscathed. Decades later, when Winnie attempts to find words for an accurate portrayal of Wen Fu's behavior during the war, she uses his own words. According to Winnie's account, during every air battle, Wen Fu deliberately flew his plane away from the fighting, nonchalantly claiming after the fighting was over that he pursued a Japanese fighter plane as it broke formation. He shrugs, "Too bad I didn't catch him" (204).

While his actions as a pilot are unconscionable and cowardly, Wen Fu's behavior as a husband and father is appallingly criminal. He repeatedly rapes his wife and abuses his children, and he is responsible for the death of his daughter, Yiku, when he refuses to send for a physician to see the desperately sick child. Wen Fu's ultimate act of villainy reverberates years later on another continent. Winnie reveals that just before her escape to America, Wen Fu traced her hiding place, beat her, tore up her divorce papers, and raped her. Pearl was conceived during that rape, and it is the truth of her parentage—the fact that her father is not kindly American Jimmy Louie but brutal Chinese Wen Fu—that she must hear from Winnie.

Winnie's oldest friend, Hulan (Helen) Kwong, is an important character in Winnie's story, both in China and in America. When Weili first meets Helen, the latter is married to Jiaguo, one of Wen Fu's fellow pilots, and despite the women's radically different personalities—unlike the submissive well-bred Weili, Hulan is a brash, confident young woman from a poor family—they become friends. Hulan's friendship with Weili becomes a relationship of long standing, dating from their years as young military wives, forced by the war to endure frequent dislocations and deprivations, and continuing to their new lives as immigrants in California's Chinese diaspora communities. Hulan, like Weili, receives an English name from an American serviceman at a dance toward the end of the war, and when she emigrates to the United States, she adopts the English name permanently. As aging women, Helen and Winnie are inextricably bound together by their uneasily shared secret, and Helen's ongoing presence in Winnie's life means that she has a significant impact on Pearl's life as well. In fact, the fear of dying from a malignant brain tumor prompts Helen into employing emotional blackmail to persuade Pearl to disclose the facts about her illness to her mother, and to force Winnie into revealing her past to her daughter. Reminding Winnie that she has been hiding from the truth for far too long, Helen announces, "Now you can come out" (76).

LITERARY DEVICES

Several familiar literary devices reappear in *The Kitchen God's Wife*, creating in the novel the same sense of place and culture that characterized *The Joy Luck Club*. Once again, food and dreams constitute major symbol and motif clusters that reinforce the novel's themes and function as narrative strategies. In addition, Tan focuses attention on three events that, through their representation of life's milestones, introduce and define the novel's conflicts and resolution.

Among the most pervasive motifs in *The Kitchen God's Wife* is food and the activities that surround its preparation and consumption. In fact, the novel opens and closes with celebratory dinners, and similar feasts and meals mark crucial events in Winnie's story. Food and its corollaries perform several significant functions: food creates the illusion of verisimilitude through the deployment of singular details that coalesce into striking visual images in the reader's mind; food serves as a characterization device; and food either links or divides past and present, traditional culture and new culture, one generation with another.

First, through verisimilitude, Amy Tan adeptly uses the imagery of food to transport her readers to the China of Weili's girlhood. Describing New Year's preparations at the home of Weili's aunt and uncle, Tan creates a culinary still life composed of the ingredients for a lavish feast: jars of kitchen staples such as peanut oil, soy sauce, and vinegar; sticky rice cakes stuffed with date paste; a wooden bucket full of fish, still alive and swimming; and ducks and chickens pecking in a courtyard. Details of the food for the New Year meals enhance the sense of celebration that Tan creates through her portrayal of the bustle and activity that pervades the entire household. Life in her uncle's house instills in Weili the sense that food is both important and symbolic, providing benefits beyond basic sustenance.

As the novel continues to follow Weili through her transition from young girl to young wife, food outlines the cultural and geographical

contexts of her life. After Weili is married, she often cooks for Wen Fu
and his fellow pilots; and because she fears that some of them might not
return after the next air raid, she devotes considerable energy and time
to ensuring that the meals are gala affairs featuring special symbolic
foods guaranteed to confer certain forms of good luck on the pilots. Her
dinners include sun-dried oysters, which are popularly said to bring
wealth and *fatsai*, the black-haired fungus that creates good fortune. Amy
Tan uses food images to re-create the city of Nanking where Weili lives
for a short time during the war. Strolling through a local market to purchase fresh ingredients for a special meal, Weili is surrounded by dozens
of tables and stalls displaying tofu in buckets, yams and turnips in heaps,
dried mushrooms in baskets, pans full of seafood, and noodles of many
varieties, including egg, rice, and wheat.

Second, food motifs also function to individualize the novel's characters through descriptions of their food preferences and eating habits. We
have noted earlier the fact that Weili's mother embodies cultural confusion with her wardrobe of Western dresses and Chinese robes. That
confusion is further reflected in her gastronomic tastes: she likes English
biscuits so much that she keeps a tin on top of her dresser, but she also
craves a certain fish called *wah-wah yu* that she remembers as "so tender,
so delicious . . . [with] scales . . . as soft and sweet as baby leaves" (95).
Early in her friendship with Hulan, Weili comments that her friend is
adept at certain kitchen tasks, but further implies that she has little re-
gard for Hulan's ability to distinguish subtle and delicate flavors and
aromas. Later, Weili criticizes Hulan for enjoying vegetables that have
been steamed so long that they are mushy and flavorless. Embedded in
Weili's derogatory remarks is the implication that Hulan is unaccustomed to the nuances of refined Chinese cuisine, but Weili inadvertently
also reveals her own need to prove that she is superior to Hulan in birth
and breeding. Unlike Hulan, who has rough rural manners, Weili is refined and sophisticated, the product of a privileged upbringing. Weili's
unacknowledged desire to best Hulan is a manifestation of her resentment that Hulan's husband, Jiaguo, outranks Wen Fu. Weili also believes
that only Jiaguo's intercession has saved Wen Fu from being court-
martialed for his cowardice during air raids and for an accident in which
a girl was killed while Wen Fu was driving a military vehicle without a
permit. Jiaguo's assistance means that Weili is forever in his debt—and
that of his wife, Hulan.

A third function of food motifs is to represent continuity and to embody the bonds between family members and friends. The engagement

party and subsequent wedding of Bao-bao, Helen's son, are notable for the elaborate meals that mark both occasions. At each dinner, family members and friends of all ages gather around tables loaded with traditional celebratory dishes, and children climb onto the laps of their elders to demand assistance with chopsticks. Interspersed with the jollity and congratulations, Winnie and Helen carry on with what appears to be their habitual behavior at family dinners—arguing about the food, about whether a pork dish might be too salty, or whether a chicken specialty is overcooked. These disagreements are not intended as genuine debates; rather they represent one of the ways through which Winnie and Helen have communicated during the long years of their friendship. Verbal sparring about food and its preparation sustained the women through their wartime experiences, and now, years later in America, they nurture their friendship and reinforce their connections through their discussions about food. Watching as Winnie and Helen make the rounds of the tables, scooping up leftovers from the wedding banquet, and arguing all the while, Pearl muses, "perhaps it is not arguing. They are remembering together, dreaming together" (410).

A fourth function of food is that it highlights the differences between the immigrant generation and their American-born children. In the long-standing culinary rivalry between Winnie and Helen, the women agree that Winnie makes the best *jiao-zi*, or steamed dumplings, while Helen specializes in chicken dishes. Unfortunately, their daughters, Pearl and Mary, have inherited none of their mothers' skill with traditional Chinese food; Pearl, in fact, admits to her mother that she never buys tofu, while Mary seems to rely on a variety of casserole recipes to feed her family and friends. The culinary gulf is still more evident in Pearl's children whose gastronomic point of reference is American fast food. At the engagement dinner, Cleo bursts into tears when she is told that the morsel of food she is chewing is jellyfish, despite Winnie's attempts to make the jellyfish familiar by suggesting that it tastes like rubber bands. At length, Helen manages to soothe the howling child by proffering some beef that she describes as tasting exactly like hamburgers from McDonald's. Immediately, Cleo stops weeping and chomps delightedly on the beef, jellyfish forgotten.

Finally, food represents memory, connecting one generation with another, and providing links between past and present, China and the United States. Recalling the day that her mother left her, Winnie tells Pearl that the morning began when a servant delivered Weili's morning bowl of *syen do jang*, and perhaps realizing that her American daughter will not recognize the Chinese words, Winnie adds hastily that *syen do jang* is the salty soy-milk soup that they purchase at a local restaurant, the same soup that Cleo devours without spilling a drop. Embedded in Winnie's reminiscence is a culinary thread that connects Shanghai and San Francisco, and links six-year-old Weili in the 1920s and three-year-old Cleo in the 1990s. For Winnie especially, certain kinds of food have specific resonances in her memory. When Helen suggests that they try a new restaurant that serves eels fried in hot oil and seasoned with chives, Winnie remembers a war-time dinner with unpleasant associations and refuses to go. Later, she asks Pearl, "Why do some memories live only on your tongue or in your nose?" (235)

Dreams constitute another major motif in *The Kitchen God's Wife*, reflecting various characters' feelings of helplessness in the face of an inexorable fate. Research into dreams has revealed that dreams are related to the emotional and psychological states of the dreamer, embodying through imagery the dreamer's unspoken conflicts and fears. In the late nineteenth century, Sigmund Freud posited the idea that dreams represent repressed desires and conflicts that cannot find expression during an individual's waking hours. Transformed into the imagery and symbolism of dreams, those desires and conflicts become more manageable, enabling the dreamer to come to terms with them. Carl Jung in the early twentieth century expanded Freud's research, describing a "collective unconscious" that encompasses not only individual dreams but also the images, patterns, and symbols shared by dreams with myth, legend, and religious ritual (see Chapter 5).

Early in *The Kitchen God's Wife*, Pearl reveals that although her father has been dead for over two decades, she continues to have vivid nightmares about his final days, a period during which she tried to deny that the father she loved was terminally ill. In her nightmares, she frantically searches for her lost father in hospital wards full of terminally ill patients, finding him at last alone and abandoned on a cot in a corner. As she approaches him in the dream, his tired old face lights up when he realizes that his daughter has finally found him and has come to take him home with her. The nightmares reflect Pearl's inability to come to terms with the loss of her adored father. At his funeral over twenty years earlier, she had been unable to grieve for her father because she could not accept the fact of his death. Her dry-eyed stoicism had angered Winnie who assumed that Pearl's silence was proof that the child did not care about her father, and Winnie had slapped Pearl. The estrangement between mother and daughter deepened, and young Pearl was left without a father and without the support of her mother. Now a grown woman with children of her own, Pearl still cannot weep for her father, and thus cannot bring closure to that part of her childhood in which he played a prominent role. In her dreams, he is simply lost and she must find him.

In her story about the worst day of her childhood, Winnie describes her memory of the dream that disturbed her sleep on the night that her mother vanished. The dream is senseless, disjointed, and lacking in narrative form, and when the child awakens, she cannot remember anything except a collection of bizarre images: a weeping fish singing a song about a mouse; a blonde girl trying on French shoes. The most indelible of the images are related to her mother:

> My mother's hair, the way my fingers wove through it only
> to discover it was not hair . . . but embroidery and jewels. My
> mother, sitting at her dressing table, combing her hair, cry-
> ing. (97)

The day before the dream, Weili has overheard her parents arguing in low voices. Her father's voice makes her want to hide, while her mother's "sounded ragged, like good cloth already torn, never able to be mended" (92). The overheard argument and her mother's strange behavior for the rest of the day are clearly manifested in the dream, which suggests a little girl's attempts to impose some order or structure on a day that has confused and frightened her.

Another dream that Winnie remembers vividly is not her own but that of a pilot named Gan, a young man who confides to Weili the dream that has disturbed his thoughts since he was a young boy during a Tiger year. In that long-ago dream, he saw a ghost who announced that he would come for Gan before the next Tiger year arrived, but that before that happened, Gan would experience nine bad fates. Gan tells Weili that eight of those fates have already happened, and that he has only four months left before the new Tiger year arrives. Gan's confession to Weili and his obsession with his dream reflect the fear and uncertainty with which the pilots and their wives face each day of the war, and his story of the dream parallels his knowledge of his impending death (the Chinese airplanes were so outdated and unreliable that death was almost certain for their pilots), reinforcing Weili's feelings of helplessness in the face of a war that seems impossible to win.

Amy Tan signposts her novel with three important family occasions— first an engagement party immediately followed by a funeral, and later a wedding. These are events that denote noteworthy passages through life, representing beginnings and endings, demarcating the temporal boundaries of the family. The novel opens with Bao-bao Kwong's engagement dinner, which brings together the Kwong and Louie families, an occasion during which seventy-three-year-old Helen Kwong draws Pearl aside into another room—ostensibly so that they can cut the cake—and announces that she, Helen, has been diagnosed with an inoperable brain tumor. "I am not telling you this so you have to worry," Helen says to the stunned Pearl, adding that she simply wants Pearl to understand why Pearl's illness can no longer be kept a secret (36). And with that, Helen extracts from Pearl the promise that Winnie will be told about Pearl's illness. At the funeral for Auntie Du the next day, Pearl, who is already vulnerable from the stress produced by her promise to Helen, is reminded of her father's funeral at which she was so numbed by grief that she could not weep, claiming (to her mother's distress), "That man in there is not my father." Pearl is still unaware that she spoke the truth in her long-ago outburst, and she cannot know that the memory that has been triggered by the sight of Auntie Du in her coffin is inextricably, mystically, tied to Pearl's promise to Helen as well as to Helen's cryptic remark that Winnie is concealing a great many secrets. But the memory suddenly allows Pearl to grieve for Jimmy Louie, and she bursts into noisy sobs. Shortly after the funeral, Helen informs Winnie that the time has come for them to reclaim the true stories of their lives, to sweep out of their lives all of the subterfuges and false stories behind which they have hidden their shared past. Demanding that Winnie make an effort to "tell everyone our true situation, how we met," Helen reasons that she wants everything set to rights before it is too late for either one of them to re-take ownership of the past. "It matters more to tell the truth," Helen says, adding that neither of them wants to go to the next world with so many lies marring their history (79).

In a sense, both the engagement party and the funeral symbolize beginnings—the party heralds Bao-bao's intention to start a new family, and the funeral is Auntie Du's send-off to the next life. In fact, the message on the banner hanging over the coffin makes the prospect of another life very clear with its inscribed hope that Auntie Du's next life will be long and prosperous. For Winnie and Pearl, the revelations that are inspired by the family gatherings signal a new chapter in their shared history, a new relationship in which they no longer have secrets from each other, and finally a new life in which their destinies are harmoniously joined.

At the end of the novel, after all of the important stories have been told, after Winnie and Pearl have shared their secrets, the Louies and the Kwongs are once again together to celebrate over a meal—this time for Bao-bao's wedding. At this event that launches Bao-bao's new family, the newlyweds are not alone in celebrating new beginnings: as Pearl and Winnie revel cautiously in their new and unaccustomed closeness, mother and daughter and Helen plan a trip together to China.

MAJOR THEMES AND ISSUES

In *The Joy Luck Club*, Tan explores the intricacies of the relationship between mothers and daughters. She continues the exploration in *The Kitchen God's Wife*, and as she has done in the earlier novel, she complicates the relationship between mother and daughter by situating them on opposite sides of a great cultural and linguistic divide. In addition, Tan raises questions about the status of women in certain cultural settings. Tan also addresses a number of other important themes and issues, among them cultural dislocations and identity confusions, marriage, the consequences of war, and the nature of friendships.

At the beginning of the novel, Pearl makes it clear that she has a problematic relationship with her mother whom she finds irritating and from whom she keeps her distance, both emotionally and geographically. Winnie is perfectly aware that the separation between herself and her daughter is not an accident of distance; she is aware also that the rift dividing them widened irreversibly on the day of Jimmy Louie's funeral when Winnie slapped Pearl because the child was unable to weep. Pearl remembers the same day, remembers also her grief that was too deep for tears because she had lost the father for whom she had been "his 'perfect Pearl' . . . not the irritation I always seemed to be with my mother" (45). Ironically, Winnie and Pearl are separated by misunderstandings: Pearl believes that her mother has always loved her brother more; Winnie is convinced that Pearl thinks that she was a bad mother; and as time goes on, it seems easier for the two women to attribute their differences to cultural factors.

The cultural contradictions inherent in the relationship between Winnie and Pearl cannot be attributed solely and glibly to the obvious fact that Winnie is an immigrant and Pearl is a second-generation native-born American. For Winnie, cultural confusion has always been a component of life, and she has learned to accept it. Young Weili is first exposed to Western culture by a mother whose love for Western adornment makes an impression on the child, who then acquires an early taste for English biscuits. Sent to live with an uncle's family, Weili immediately notices that her new home has two identities: Old East, built as a one-storied structure with important rooms facing east in the Chinese style, and New West, a two-storied chimneyed building, added when the family became wealthy by trading with foreigners.

As she narrates her story to Pearl, Winnie constantly juxtaposes East and West, always emphasizing the differences between the two. "Maybe it was 1937 by the Western calendar," she remarks, trying to fix the date of an important event (112). Another time, she makes sure that Pearl understands clearly that the traditional Chinese New Year celebration differs tremendously from the American festivities. Pearl, being American-born and educated, does not have two clear points of reference as her mother does, and Winnie's constant references to things Chinese frustrate Pearl who complains that her mother can be infuriating with her "various hypotheses, the way religion, medicine, and superstition all merge with her own beliefs" (29). Adding that Winnie is convinced that nothing is ever an accident, Pearl compares Winnie to "a Chinese version of Freud or worse" (29). Because she is so thoroughly a contemporary American woman, Pearl is irked by her mother's demand that she participate in family traditions that to her are simply burdensome. Winnie, for her part, seems baffled by her inability to approach rapport with her daughter, and her attempts to start conversations end up simply sounding to Pearl like criticism.

What Pearl does not know—and what she discovers by the end of the novel—is that Winnie is a much more complicated individual than her children could possibly have imagined. In fact, Pearl does not truly know her mother or her mother's story, and until she receives that knowledge, she will continue to misinterpret Winnie's words and actions as simply the peculiarities of an elderly Chinese woman.

Another theme that is addressed in *The Kitchen God's Wife* is the position of women in severely patriarchal cultures. Through Winnie's story about life as Jiang Weili, Amy Tan explores what it meant to be a woman in Chinese society before and during World War II. Weili is the product of a culture that privileges the Confucian ideal, raising women to be passive and silent in their roles as daughters, wives, and mothers. Her story, which has strong resonances with the old European tale of Patient Griselda, reveals the suffering of a woman whose brutish husband abuses her privately and publicly while the couple's friends and acquaintances (and, by extension, the entire culture that has shaped them) pretend that nothing is amiss. Most disturbing to Western readers is the fact that Weili's closest women friends—Hulan and Auntie Du—collude with Weili's husband in his persecution of his wife. Both women stand silently by when Wen Fu forces Weili into the degrading position of kneeling before him to beg for forgiveness; worse still, both women believe Wen Fu when he promises earnestly that he will be kind to Weili if they reveal to him where she is hiding. Tan seems to be implying that much cultural conditioning can be so thorough and its effects so ingrained that even the members of victimized classes accept their oppression and abuse as a fact of their lives, and they inadvertently perpetuate their own victimization through their passivity and refusal to speak out.

Not until Weili meets the American, Jimmy Louie, is she able to break away from the cultural oppression under which she has lived. As Jimmy's lover and then later as his wife, she begins to understand that marriage can be the genuine union of two hearts and minds, and not simply an economic merger or a legal institution designed to produce male heirs for the husband's family. More importantly, Weili learns that marital sex is not always rape and does not have to be painful or degrading. She discovers—to her surprise—that making love with the right man is a joyful experience. Through Jimmy, she is introduced to passionate love and tender affection; with him she finds the happiness that has eluded her for most of her life.

A third theme that Amy Tan addresses in the novel is the construction of identity. As a young woman in pre-war China, Weili must inhabit an identity that has been codified by her culture for centuries. Before she is married, she is the daughter of one of the wealthiest Shanghai tycoons and the niece of the richest man on an island off the coast of Shanghai. After her marriage, she becomes the wife of a pilot in China's fledgling air force, and later the mother of Yiku and Danru. In each case, she is identified through her role in a traditional relationship. Although Weili is an intelligent and resourceful woman who exhibits an unusual tendency to question the status quo, she engages in that questioning only in her mind. And because her roles are so rigidly defined, she is not confronted with the need to identify to herself who Jiang Weili truly is—until her marriage collapses and she meets and falls in love with Jimmy Louie.

Weili's transformation begins when Jimmy christens her ''Winnie'' at the American dance during which he assigns English names to dozens of other young Chinese party goers. Unconnected with either her father or her husband, the new name signals a new woman and a new beginning. By giving permission for Weili to marry Wen Fu, her father has indicated that she means little to him and that he is willing to give her away to a man whom he knows to be a fraud. Wen Fu, through his abuse and infidelity, has already repudiated Weili. All of her children are dead. Weili is, in fact, completely disconnected from her old life, and when she embraces the name "Winnie," she relinquishes her identity as a woman in Confucian China and steps into a new role as an immigrant woman in America. Winnie is immune to the cultural restrictions that bind Weili, but with that new name and its implied new role come unfamiliar challenges and barriers.

As she begins to rebuild her life in the United States, Winnie soon discovers that she has once again become anonymous. None of her family credentials are important in her adopted country, and in her new life as in the old, she is identified by her relationship to another individual— she is the wife of James Louie, minister, and she is the mother of two American children. While she was in China, her limited English had set her above her peers who knew one or two words at best, but in California, her English sets her apart as a recent immigrant, as marginal and therefore inconsequential. Compounding the linguistic problem is the fact that Winnie has not completely divested herself of her past; she hides from her husband and her daughter a painful secret that affects them both. Her silence on the matter defines her identity in ways that go beyond her immediate family. Because she must keep her counsel about her secret, she is forced to pretend that Helen is her sister-in-law, once married to a mythical brother who died during the war. In some very crucial ways, Winnie's American identity is a deliberately false construct, an artificial role that limits her almost as definitively as did the submissive roles that she played as Jiang Weili.

Winnie's anonymity—a form of unstable identity—results from a failure of translation. We have already noted that Weili is intelligent, perceptive, and strong—she has to be to survive the horror of her marriage with her mind and heart intact. As Winnie, she has not lost those qualities; but they have been obscured in the wholesale revision that reinvents Weili as Winnie. With a few strokes of a pen, Jimmy Louie transforms Weili, wife of Wen Fu, into Winnie Louie, wife of American citizen, James Louie. The action creates a necessary fiction, one that will allow Weili to escape China; but unfortunately, instead of translating Weili's characteristics into an American incarnation, Jimmy inadvertently erases Jiang Weili, replacing her with a newly minted stranger. Thus for most of her American life, Winnie is forced—by the lie that brought her to America, and by her shame about the last degradation she has had to endure—to suppress Weili and the story of her life. Winnie's condition is similar to that endured by Ying-ying St. Clair in *The Joy Luck Club*. Both women are reinvented by well-meaning adoring American husbands whose only thought is to get their beloved wives out of China and into the United States. In each case, the reinvention eradicates the evidence of an earlier persona. For Ying-ying, the erasure is more profound; Clifford St. Clair alters his wife's birth date, transforming her from a woman born in a Tiger year into a stranger born in a Dragon year. Lacking Winnie's inner fire, Ying-ying simply retreats into herself, becoming a silent ghost-like presence; and because she tells her story in an interior monologue, her reintegration with her self remains incomplete. By contrast, Winnie, at the conclusion of *The Kitchen God's Wife*, is whole. By telling her story—speaking aloud the events of Weili's life, and putting into words Weili's thoughts and feelings—Winnie is able to effect the translation of Weili into Winnie. Like the best translations, Winnie's story preserves exactly the essence and rhythms, as well as the underlying structure and aesthetic shape of the original. Winnie has reclaimed herself, but more than that, she has given her daughter a history that Pearl must, in her turn, translate into the story of her own life.

ALTERNATE READING: FEMINIST

Feminist Criticism

Feminist criticism is not a monolithic single approach to literary analysis or a rigidly codified methodology, but rather an attitude that derives from concern about social and cultural attitudes about and toward women. Arlyn Diamond and Lee Edwards point out that whereas feminists subscribe to a shared core of beliefs, feminist criticism—which employs gender as a focal point of literary analysis—"can turn a wide variety of existing techniques to its own ends" (xiv). In other words, feminist criticism is interdisciplinary, intradisciplinary, and intercultural, and its purpose is to examine literary and artistic texts through a gendered lens that illuminates the imbalance of power between men and women.

At its most basic, feminist criticism of literature is shaped by its concern with literary representations of gender and power, by its interrogation of a canon that has been shaped not only by predominantly male values but also through the exclusion of the female voice. And despite the variety of methodologies employed by feminist critics, they have in common a number of assumptions and beliefs about culturally inscribed gender roles:

> [A]ll feminists, I would argue, would agree that women are not automatically or necessarily inferior to men, that role models for females and males in the current Western societies are inadequate, that equal rights for women are necessary, that it is unclear what by nature either men or women are, that it is a matter for empirical investigation to ascertain what differences follow from the obvious physiological ones, that in these empirical investigations the hypotheses one employs are themselves open to question, revision, or replacement. (9)

Although the feminist movement has had a long history that goes back centuries, feminist criticism first emerged as a field of academic inquiry in the 1960s through the efforts of women who were predominantly of the academic and literary establishment. During the decades that followed, feminist criticism gradually developed through several distinct stages into a discipline.

In its formative years, feminist criticism focused on exposing the misogyny that had been institutionalized in literary study, the exclusion of women from literary history, and the subordination of women in the literary canon. Feminist critics examined the canon, illuminating the gaps in literary history, noting the absence of women as authors and as subjects, and seeking to expose the patriarchal suppression of women's voices. Early feminist critics argued that literature displayed pervasive narrative patterns that privileged men and devalued women; and they argued further that those patterns had become so entrenched that they reinforced and thus perpetuated the silencing of women.

The second phase of development of feminist criticism involved the discovery or recovery—and reading—of literary texts by women writers whose work had suffered from neglect or the obscurity that accompanies exclusion from the canon. This literary archaeology resulted in the retrieval of thousands of works of major historical and artistic merit, works that had, in fact, been well-received at their first publication but had eventually been erased from literary history through the systematic—if unacknowledged—privileging of the artifacts and productions of a patriarchal culture. In this phase of development, which revealed that women have a coherent and significant literary tradition of their own, feminist critics and literary historians effected important revisions to the literary canon as well as to the study of literature.

In its maturity, feminist criticism has progressed beyond its original demand for recognition of the value of women's writing, beyond the retrieval of forgotten or neglected texts, to a focus on the basic concepts that underlie literary and cultural analysis. With this focus have come certain demands: that widely accepted cultural and theoretical assumptions about the acts of writing and reading be revised to include female experience; and that literary texts be interrogated to unmask the ways in which gender and sexuality are constructed in and through literature.

Feminist criticism is, therefore, an orientation, a way of reading the world that employs a variety of strategies and theoretical positions. Like cultural criticism to which it is closely related, feminist criticism draws from a wide range of disciplines, fields of study, and approaches, including anthropology, history, linguistics, literary theory, Marxism, psychoanalysis, and sociology.

One way of reading *The Kitchen God's Wife* as a feminist text would be to examine the novel as the record of a woman's journey from silence to full voice through the vehicle of storytelling, a performance that is widely considered to be a female act. In writing Winnie's life, Amy Tan exposes the layers of silence under which are buried the forgotten stories of women like Winnie—like Tan's own mother. As Winnie recounts her story in the novel, she shapes and thus reclaims her life, breaking the long silence that has marked her existence since that long-ago day when her mother vanished, never to be mentioned by anyone again.

Feminist critics have noted several kinds of silences, both self-imposed and externally sanctioned. Silence is the absence of voice, of words or phrases, or even topics, that one is forbidden (by discretion or by express injunction) to mention or is forced to avoid. Silence can result from feelings of shame, inadequacy, or unworthiness; from social or cultural conditioning; from the inability to speak a language. Silence also can result from the existence of so many variations of a story that the truth is obscured or remains unsaid. For many women, silence is a strategy for coping—a way to avoid pain or to evade confrontation or dealing with the unpleasant, a technique for negotiating grief, anger, or shame.

The effects of silence on a woman are many and varied: misunderstanding, loneliness and isolation, erasure and invisibility, depression, madness, even death. Silence between women negates the possibility of companionship, friendship, and trust. Silence between mother and daughter deprives both of a shared history and a common emotional language, rendering them virtual strangers. A woman without a voice cannot claim herself or her life; moreover, by not speaking her own story, she allows that story to be constructed by someone else.

The Kitchen God's Wife is about women's silences, and about the ways through which women can empower themselves to break those silences. At the center of the novel is the palpable heavy silence between Winnie Louie and her daughter Pearl. For almost forty years, Winnie has not spoken the truth about her life in China, and has, in fact, referred to that life only obliquely and only in the presence of Helen, the friend who has been complicitous in Winnie's silence. In fact, Helen is also implicated in perpetuating the conspiracy of silence about Pearl's multiple sclerosis; and ultimately, Helen becomes the catalyst that sends both Winnie and Pearl on the journey toward reclaiming their voices.

Winnie is afflicted with a profound voicelessness. Her silence simultaneously is the product of her upbringing, the consequence of an abusive marriage, and the by-product of her shame. In the company of so many traditionally raised Chinese women of her generation, Winnie has been socialized by her culture into silence:

> Women of well-to-do families, whether aristocratic, bureaucratic, or merchant, though often educated and literate, nevertheless lived a generally restricted life fulfilling their prescribed roles of wife, mother, daughter-in-law, and mother-in-law. . . . A woman's primary tasks were to perform her domestic duties, take care of her husband, children, and elders, and ensure the future of her husband's lineage by giving birth to male children. (Duke xi)

As an upper-class female in pre-republic China, Weili has been raised according to centuries-old Confucian philosophy, which recognizes three bonds of subordination and loyalty that are fundamental to a properly functioning state: the submission of a minister to the ruling prince, of a son to his father, and of a wife to her husband. Confucius, in fact, dismissed women as similar only to slaves and children. His followers reiterated his philosophy more explicitly in the centuries that followed, suggesting, for instance, that women should be barred from any participation in government, and asserting that education had a negative effect on women, transforming them into bored and discontented individuals who then became unfit wives and mothers (Ling 3).

A young woman like Weili would have been taught to obey the Three Obediences and Four Virtues, a code of conduct that governed Chinese women's lives from the first century A.D. into the twentieth century:

> The Three Obediences enjoined a woman to obey her father before marriage, her husband after marriage, and her eldest son after her husband's death. The Four Virtues decreed that she be chaste; her conversation courteous and not gossipy; her deportment graceful but not extravagant; her leisure spent in perfecting her needlework and tapestry for beautifying the home. (3)

Implicit in the code is the idea that women should be silent, reticent, retiring, and submissive before the men in their lives. Bound by that code, Jiang Weili diligently schools herself to think only of Wen Fu's needs and wants regardless of the cost to her body and soul. In her mind, however, she silently, voicelessly questions herself and her actions, wondering what she might have done to deserve her plight.

During the long war years, Weili focuses her energies on fulfilling her obligations as a wife and mother, spending her dowry money on luxury food items to entertain Wen Fu's friends, submitting to her husband's rough assaults on her body, enduring his taunts and accusations. At the beginning of the marriage, she shows some of her natural spirit, but after she becomes the object of Wen Fu's vicious temper too many times, she learns to keep her counsel and say nothing. Winnie tells Pearl about being raised "never to criticize men or the society they ruled, or Confucius" (257). Although she remains silent when their servant girl leaves, Weili is well aware that the girl has been raped repeatedly by Wen Fu; but when Weili hears the news that the girl has died because of a botched abortion, she forgets to be silent and taxes Wen Fu with her knowledge. He responds by beating their six-month-old baby, Yiku, until the child curls up in pain. The traumatized child never learns to speak; in fact, she dies at a year and a half without ever having said a word. Thus Wen Fu renders his daughter voiceless, and her story is unspoken until Winnie breaks her silence decades later. The deaths of Yiku and Danru, Weili's little son, as well as Mochou who is stillborn, and the babies that Weili forces herself to abort, further silence her; and her final attempt to assert herself only results in Wen Fu's last and worst assault on her body.

So shamed and humiliated is Weili by the time she leaves China that she has been unable to speak of her last dreadful weeks in China, nor has she ever told the full story of her marriage to her daughter.

The silence that cloaks Pearl is not as profound or multifaceted as her mother's is, but Pearl's speechlessness is as debilitating as the illness that she conceals from her mother. Unlike Winnie, whose silence obscures the past, Pearl attempts to negate the present. She refuses her cousin Mary's attempts to be supportive, driving Mary into extreme self-consciousness about words and actions that might suggest that Pearl is not well. Between Pearl and her husband Phil, the silence takes the form of near-denial that she has a degenerative disorder, which they refer to obliquely as her "medical condition." They do not mention the fact that their new house is a one-story structure with wide hallways that can accommodate a wheelchair if necessary. They speak about her illness in their own private code. And although Pearl has instigated the silence that now surrounds her, she finds it unnerving that Phil can so completely pretend that their life is normal, while she—who desires that normalcy more than he does—frets in silence, unable to articulate her needs or the reasons for her frustrations. "[Now] I can't tell him what I really feel . . . the worst part is when I remember . . . that I am living in a limbo land called remission" (28). Compounding the isolation that Pearl feels because she can no longer discuss her condition with Phil is her growing disquiet at having kept the secret from her mother for seven years. Pearl's silence deprives her of the emotional support that she craves from the two people from whom she most needs it. Moreover, she is consumed with guilt because Winnie is the only member of their extended family who remains unaware of the secret and its implications.

Both Winnie and Pearl must reclaim their voices. Because each woman's silence is an elemental factor of her relationship with the other, they must break their silences together and together they must speak aloud those thoughts and stories that they have concealed for so long. Only as they share their lives with each other will they be able to repair the breach between them that has widened steadily since Jimmy Louie died.

For Winnie, the act of rupturing the silence in which her voice is wrapped is a complicated process because she is doubly voiceless. In her past, in the ancestral Confucian culture of her homeland, she was silenced because of her gender; in her American present, she is silenced by a dominant culture that marginalizes immigrants like her. Winnie's inability to tell her story is caused not only by the shame that she still carries with her from the disaster of her first marriage, but also by her knowledge that she does not know how to speak like anyone other than an immigrant. Even her thoroughly American daughter unthinkingly contributes to Winnie's muteness by insisting almost priggishly that Winnie learn to tell her friends that Pearl is a "speech and language clinician for children with moderate to severe communicative disorders" (82). Unable to twist her tongue around the alien polysyllabic terminology, Winnie worries that her daughter will believe her to be unintelligent or slow-witted. Winnie's fear is a symptom of her powerlessness, which is the most insidiously destructive consequence of her silence; for if the absence of a voice bars access to power, the lack of power, in turn, renders an individual mute.

Storytelling is Winnie's strategy for revisiting the past to reclaim her voice. Long ago, on the long evacuation from Nanking into the mountains, Weili and Hulan had invented stories to keep their spirits up and to maintain their emotional strength on the grueling journey. Similarly, as Winnie carefully and slowly remembers and then articulates the shaping events of her life, she progresses on the journey toward verbal authority and eloquence. As the author of her story, she has the power to pass on that story to her daughter, and that story becomes an emotional lifeline between mother and daughter. Just as Winnie has shared not only her own life but also that of her mother, so will Pearl, one day, recount Winnie's stories to Tessa and Cleo, thus ensuring an unbroken link from Winnie's mother to Winnie's granddaughters.

As she speaks aloud what is, in essence, her autobiography, Winnie re-shapes her perceptions and analyzes the significance of crucial events, and, in retrospect, she admits to herself that she changed during her marriage. She learned to silence herself. "Can you imagine how innocent I was?" (151), she asks as she concludes the story of her wedding. She tells Pearl that at her wedding she was still dreaming of celebrations and festivities that she would orchestrate, she was fantasizing of happiness with her new husband. Throughout her narrative, Winnie reflects on the transformations that she undergoes at each milestone of that marriage. By the time her second daughter is born, Weili has learned to silence the truth, and when Wen Fu's bad temper terrifies the baby, Weili dissembles, crooning to the crying child that the belligerent man is a stranger and not the child's father who is a kind and gentle man. Soon after that incident, on learning what Wen Fu has done to their servant girl, Weili recalls being told as a child never to create a large problem by complaining about a small one, and she pays the servant to leave. To Pearl, Winnie says that she consciously chose silence and inaction: "I made myself blind [and] . . . deaf" (260). If Weili has become outwardly a silent, accepting, uncomplaining wife to Wen Fu, inwardly she is seething. Ordered by him to crouch on the floor and beg for his forgiveness in front of their dinner guests, Weili obeys, but in her mind she wonders why none of the onlookers volunteers to come to her rescue: "Why do they stand there, as if I were truly wrong?" (253). Clearly, Wen Fu—despite his problems—is not solely to blame for Weili's oppression. She is silenced not only by her husband, but also by the friends who allow him to continue his brutal and dehumanizing treatment of her. Winnie, years later, cannot erase the memory of her friends' passive participation in her degradation, but as she tells her story, she begins to understand and finally to withhold condemnation, concluding at last that she cannot blame Helen for her seeming complicity with Wen Fu during the war years: "She was scared. . . . But I still can't forget" (253).

The point, of course, is not that Winnie should forget but that she reclaim the self that has been silenced. Through stories, Winnie re-imagines her past and comes to terms with it, and she relives her traumatic history, transforming it into an allegory of the human spirit's ability to survive the worst of circumstances. Winnie sees, finally, not only unmitigated tragedy and loss, but also her own resilience and courage and inner strength. Her story is her gift to her daughter; and the three traits that she has uncovered and acknowledged to herself are her enduring legacy to that daughter and her children, Winnie's grandchildren.

Encouraged by Winnie's honesty and emboldened by the example of a woman who has triumphed over far more than multiple sclerosis, Pearl finds the courage to share her own secret with her mother. And although, as Robb Forman Dew has noted, "the consequences the two women endure are simply not equally horrific" (9), Pearl's admission has given Winnie the gift of a new alliance and a new battle—one that they can fight together as friends instead of strangers.

In the last scene of the novel, Winnie presents Pearl with a statue for the little red altar temple that Pearl has inherited from Grand Auntie Du. The statue represents the once-silent and forgiving Kitchen God's Wife, a woman whom Winnie has canonized as the protector of women who are learning to break their silences. Caroline Ong points out the implications of Winnie's action:

> There is no such deity among the heavenly pantheon: the only
> recognized goddesses are those with suitable womanly qual-

ities such as Mercy and Love. Winnie is rewriting the ending
to a centuries-old legend so that justice can finally be served.
(20)

As Pearl weeps, overcome with emotion at the significance of her
mother's gift to her, Winnie's instructions enjoin the younger woman to
speech. Winnie tells Pearl to unburden her soul to the Kitchen God's
Wife, who is prepared to listen and then help. "She will wash away
everything sad with her tears. . . . See her name: Lady Sorrowfree, happiness winning over bitterness, no regrets in this world" (415).

5

The Hundred Secret Senses
(1995)

Having explored the dynamics of the mother-daughter relationship in her first two novels, Amy Tan turns to the sisterly bond in her third, *The Hundred Secret Senses*, published in 1995. Reviews for the new novel were mixed; some commentators described it as Tan's best work while others found fault with either Tan's focus on supernatural elements or with the novel's conclusion. Most reviewers did, however, acknowledge Tan's gift for storytelling, and many pointed out that Kwan in *Secret Senses* is one of Tan's most original and best character creations.

Readers familiar with Tan's work will immediately recognize in *The Hundred Secret Senses* a number of distinctive Tan trademarks: a strong sense of place, a many-layered narrative, family secrets, generational conflict, Chinese lore and history, and an engrossing story. Employing multiple settings—twentieth-century San Francisco and Changmian, China, as well as nineteenth-century China during the final years of the Taiping Rebellion—Amy Tan spins out *The Hundred Secret Senses* across two centuries and two continents, unraveling the mysteriously inter-woven stories of Olivia Bishop and her half sister, Li Kwan, and Nelly Banner and her "loyal friend" Nunumu.

The Hundred Secret Senses is a novel of contrasts—the story of two sisters, two cultures, two lives, two centuries linked by loyalties and betrayals, love and loss, life and death. At the heart of the novel is the complex and uneasy relationship between California-born Olivia and her much older Chinese-born half-sister, Kwan, who comes to America when she is eighteen years old. The daughter of Jack Yee and his discarded first wife, Kwan is markedly Chinese, while Olivia, whose mother is Jack Yee's second—and American—wife, is so definitively American that her idea of ethnic food is take-out Chinese cuisine. Perhaps because she is already an adult when she emigrates, Kwan never truly assimilates into American culture, although she takes an unrestrained delight in all things American. Unfortunately, Olivia as a child is frequently mortified by her unusual new sister who asks too many odd questions, never learns to speak fluent English, and engulfs her with loyalty and devotion combined with a goofy determination to maneuver Olivia into sharing all of her secrets.

The most unnerving of those secrets is Kwan's unshakeable belief that she is gifted with *yin eyes*, a term that she employs (and that Amy Tan invented) to explain her frequent conversations with people who are already dead and who inhabit an otherworldly existence that she calls "the World of Yin" (another Tan invention). Disturbed by Kwan's non-chalant communication with ghosts, Olivia nevertheless grows up half-listening, but very much against her will, to Kwan's stories about *yin* people and a previous life in nineteenth-century China. Although Olivia claims not to believe in the *yin* people, she has actually seen (or perhaps dreamed vividly about) at least one *yin* person when she was a child; and she has no compunction about enlisting their aid through Kwan's mediation in her campaign to marry Simon Bishop. As an adult, Olivia tries to distance herself from Kwan and her tales, but Kwan's stories do not disappear with time. In fact, as Kwan approaches her fiftieth birth-day, her compulsion to talk about the *yin* people and her life in China increases tremendously, and Olivia finds herself bombarded with more stories and with snippets of reminiscences that Kwan seems to expect her mystified sister to "remember" or at least recognize somehow.

When the Bishop marriage disintegrates after seventeen years, Kwan begins to insist that she and her *yin* friends believe that Olivia and Simon should put behind them their divorce plans and instead work toward reconciliation. Finally, Kwan maneuvers the estranged pair into accom-panying her to China to visit the village of her childhood and adoles-cence. Despite their misgivings about the journey, Olivia and Simon agree to go, and when they arrive in Kwan's home village of Changmian, they are almost instantly catapulted into an alien landscape in which the dominant features are both unrecognizably strange and disturbingly fa-miliar to Olivia. In this disorienting setting, she and Simon are forced to confront the hidden resentments and disguised angers that have destroyed their marriage.

Interwoven with Olivia's story is Kwan's intermittent but compelling series of narratives of her past life as a girl named Nunumu in the nineteenth century during which she claims that she worked as a servant in a household of English missionaries. Central to that life was the close friendship that developed between Nunumu and Miss Banner, whose affair with a bogus American general puts the entire group of foreigners in danger, and whose later love for a half-Chinese–half-American interpreter leads to her death as well as that of the faithful Nunumu.

Kwan's need to reconcile past and present, and her desire to connect her lives, serve as the catalyst for the revelation of secrets, the articulation of unspoken pain, the reaffirmation of love and—at the end—the payment of old debts of loyalty. And although Kwan mysteriously disappears before Olivia's and Simon's daughter is born, the reader is left with the suggestion that the child is Kwan's gift to the couple as well as a reminder of Kwan's place in their history.

PLOT DEVELOPMENT

The plot of *The Hundred Secret Senses* follows two narrative threads: Olivia's search for an integrated self, and Kwan's desire to undo the damage of a century-old mistake. Although the two are closely related, the connections between them do not immediately become obvious but emerge gradually as elements of each plot come to light and reveal echoes of the other.

Borrowing a technique from the classical epic, Amy Tan begins the novel *in medias res*, or—colloquially translated—in the middle of the action. Over a century earlier in China, Kwan—with the very best intentions—told a lie, fabricating a story that had the unforeseen effect of disrupting the lives of two people and abruptly terminating the romance that had begun between them. The plot that has Kwan at its center is the history of her previous existence as Nunumu; the events of her life gradually reveal the incidents that lead inexorably toward the mistake that separates Miss Banner and Yiban. Now in California, Kwan is devoting her energies to the cause of rectifying her mistake and reuniting the lovers. Meanwhile, in the narrative of Olivia's efforts to discover what she wants her life to become, Olivia and Simon already are separated and have initiated the legal transactions that will lead to divorce.

Both women tell their stories, but whereas Olivia's narratives suggest interior monologues with a pervasive component of self-questioning and no identifiable audience, Kwan's stories—which are embedded in Olivia's—are clearly addressed to Olivia.

As Olivia sorts through the emotional chaos resulting from her separation from Simon, she repeatedly is reminded of the events of their courtship, the early years of their marriage, and their more recent attempts to revive the companionship they felt when they were younger. Because Simon was and is her first and only love, Olivia is not dealing well with the break-up of her marriage, and Kwan, who is still the protective older sister although they are both adults, worries constantly about Olivia, inviting her to dinner, dropping in for brief visits, offering the opinion that the separation is a mistake and that Olivia and Simon should reconcile. In the first half of the novel, each overture by Kwan prompts Olivia to remember a story that Kwan has told her, and each story told by Kwan in turn somehow returns the narrative to Olivia's emotional dilemma. With each new story, the outlines of connections become clearer. Initially, it appears that Kwan wants to bring the couple back together because she was responsible for the evening during which Elza—a *yin* person and Simon's first love who had been dead for a while—supposedly told Simon to forget her and to find happiness with Olivia. But Kwan's stories and everyday conversation are laced with oblique references to her belief that the rightness of Olivia's and Simon's union was determined by events in the distant past, and eventually Kwan manages to persuade Simon and Olivia to join her on a trip to China where, she points out mysteriously, they will discover the true pattern of their lives.

During the China trip, Olivia's and Kwan's narratives abruptly change. Removed from the familiar and confronted with a new culture, Olivia curtails her litany of past rejections and begins instead to detail events as they happen; and because she is in China, Olivia no longer has to rely on her memory of Kwan's stories—China is all around her to be experienced. Kwan, for her part, increases the number and frequency of her stories about Nunumu and Miss Banner, adding stories that Olivia has never heard—for instance, the story of Yiban and the last days in the Ghost Merchant's house, or the tale of the flight to the mountains. Early in the novel, Kwan's stories emerge as Olivia's memories, but in the final chapters, Kwan tells her stories in the immediate present. Gone is the slow gentle rhythm of memory; each tale now is urgent, immediate, triggered by the sight of a mountain or the taste of a special dish or, ultimately, the very palpable presence of a music box that Kwan claims to have hidden in a cave over a century earlier. Kwan's final stories clarify connections: Olivia and Simon are Miss Banner and Yiban, and Kwan has brought them to Changmian to reunite them. The novel ends with an epilogue narrated by Olivia. She and Simon are working toward reconciliation. More important, they have a daughter who was conceived in China, and who is—Olivia firmly believes—Kwan's final gift to them.

NARRATIVE STRATEGIES

Tan employs the juxtaposition of past and present as a narrative device for her story of the indestructibility of love and loyalty. Past and present are so closely interrelated that Olivia ultimately admits to being occasionally confused about whether an event actually occurred or is merely an episode in one of Kwan's frequently recounted stories. Toward the end of the novel, as Olivia and Kwan turn over the contents of the ancient music box that the latter says she hid in a cave more than a hundred years earlier, Olivia's logical mind races from one explanation to another. Always the rational American woman of the 1990s, Olivia is inclined to doubt what her senses suggest; nevertheless, she cannot dismiss the fact of Kwan's unflinching candor. In their time together, Olivia has never known Kwan to lie; in fact, Kwan says only what she truly believes to be true. And although Olivia knows that she should believe Kwan even now, another question surfaces: "[I]f I believe what she says, does that mean I now believe she has *yin* eyes?" (320). At that moment, Olivia realizes what she has known, has in fact believed all along—since childhood—that Kwan does remember events, the memory of which defies rational explanation.

Events in the past clearly and significantly influence the lives of both Olivia and Kwan. They are sisters, thanks to Jack Yee's two marriages and the shameful act of thievery that provided him with the wherewithal to abandon a wife and child, to discard an identity, and to begin a new life and new family in America. Through her conversations with her *yin* friends about Olivia's marital problems, Kwan bridges the chronological gap between her two lives, and Olivia is forced to endure advice and comments on her marriage from a certain Lao Lu, a friend of Kwan's from the Taiping days in the Ghost Merchant's house. Not even Olivia's marriage is immune to the influence of the past: after nearly two decades of marriage, Simon still appears to be obsessed with his first love who was killed in an avalanche.

During the visit to China, Kwan becomes more and more insistent that she and Olivia have had a previous life together, and when the sisters are together on the mountain, Olivia begins to half believe that she does indeed recognize in her present circumstances a series of strong resonances from another time. Whether these frissons of memory are remnants of Kwan's stories or genuine recollections from Olivia's past is immaterial. What is clear is that Olivia finds the more distinctive elements of the Guilin landscape disturbingly familiar.

Present and past finally collide on a rain-drenched mountain just beyond Changmian. Assailed from all directions by a cascade of sensory and emotional stimuli (Kwan's final story about her last hours in the nineteenth century, a hilly landscape that possesses a dreamlike familiarity combined with jarring strangeness, Simon's disappearance into the cold mist, Kwan's rediscovery of the music box that she last saw when she was Nunumu, and finally Kwan's revelation of the truth about Simon and Elza), Olivia is drawn into an admission that her history with Kwan could have begun near this mountain in an earlier century. It remains only for Olivia to unearth the jars full of duck eggs that Kwan says Nunumu buried during the Taiping troubles. As Olivia holds the ancient crumbling duck eggs in her cupped hands, the act liberates her from the doubts that have undermined all of her relationships. And although Kwan vanishes into the Changmian caves and is never found despite an intensive and protracted search, Olivia believes that the daughter who is born to her and Simon nine months later is a gift from Kwan. The child is not Kwan, exactly, but she is connected with Kwan in some mysterious way—and in that little girl, the past and the present are fused into wholeness and the future.

As she does in her other novels, Tan relies on formal storytelling as a narrative strategy in *The Hundred Secret Senses*. Both Kwan's nineteenth-century existence as Nunumu and her twentieth-century childhood in Changmian before her emigration to America emerge through narrative set pieces that Kwan performs as though they are legends or folktales, artifacts of an oral tradition that she feels impelled to pass on to Olivia who is her captive audience.

Tan uses the flashback technique to superb effect in the novel. New words, chance remarks, familiar objects and mementos, the taste of traditional Chinese dishes, and celebrations trigger Kwan's recollections, prompting her to narrate vignettes, brief tales, events, the particulars of specific episodes in her former lives. In one instance, when she overhears the neighborhood children referring to her as "a retard" and forces Olivia to define the word, Kwan suddenly is reminded of Miss Banner's early attempts to speak Chinese, and she tells Olivia that Nunumu initially thought that Miss Banner's inability to speak or understand Chinese indicated a lack of intelligence. On occasion, Kwan says, Nunumu actually laughed at Miss Banner's feeble attempts to converse in the vernacular. The memory prompts Kwan immediately to launch into an account of Miss Banner's first garbled description of her early life. Because Miss Banner cannot speak adequate Chinese, she ends up thoroughly confusing Nunumu by telling an impossibly surrealistic story about her origins, but Nunumu's patience with her mistress eventually results in her success at teaching Miss Banner how to view the world "exactly as a Chinese person" would (49).

By providing multiple versions of and varying perspectives on events that are central to the novel, Tan explores the ways through which storytellers create meaning on many levels and from different points of view. In some cases, the plurality of versions is the inadvertent result of misunderstandings, incomplete information, or even partial fabrication; in other cases, variant editions of a story signal the storyteller's intent to deceive. Tan seems to be suggesting that the truth exists both in each version of a story and somewhere in the unspoken narrative or in the spaces between stories.

A hallmark of *The Hundred Secret Senses* is the novel's precarious position somewhere between the real and the surreal, between the prosaic and the magical. When Kwan as Nunumu first hears Miss Banner's life story told in fractured stumbling Chinese, she forms the impression that Miss Banner has come from a peculiarly skewed and topsy-turvy universe. Miss Banner's little brothers chase a chicken into a deep hole and fall all the way to the other side of the world; her father picks scented money that grows like flowers and makes people happy; her mother puffs out her neck like a rooster, calls for her sons, and climbs down the hole that has swallowed them. After her mother's disappearance, Miss Banner's father takes her first to a palace governed by little Jesuses, and later to an island ruled by mad dogs. At length, the father vanishes and Miss Banner lives with a succession of uncles including one who cuts off pieces of China and sails off on a floating island. The reality—which Kwan learns after Miss Banner becomes more fluent in Chinese—is that Miss Banner's brothers died of chicken pox and her mother of a goiter disease; her father was an opium trader who put her in a school for

Jesus-worshipping children in India; father and daughter left India for Malacca; and the uncles were actually a series of lovers. Tan's clever juxtaposition of fact and whimsy complements the surrealism that pervades the entire novel and validates for the reader the simultaneous existence of twentieth century and nineteenth century, Chinese and American, Kwan and Nunumu, and the *yin* people in Tan's fictional universe.

Tan also employs multiple versions of a story to create uncertainty and to describe a world in which no definite answers are possible. Jack Yee, the shadowy father that Kwan and Olivia barely remember, is an enigma to both daughters, but for different reasons. In Olivia's version of Jack's story—passed on to her by the American-born adults in the family—Jack was a good-looking university student in Guilin who was forced to marry a young market vendor when she became pregnant with his child. Five years later, when his wife died of a lung disease, the grief-stricken Jack left his young daughter with an aunt and went to Hong Kong to begin a new life. Before he could send for his beloved daughter, the Communist takeover in China destroyed all hope for a reunion between father and child, and the despondent Jack emigrated to America. Kwan's arrival replaces the sad story with an even more disturbing one. According to Kwan, her mother did not die of a lung disease; she died of "heartsickness" when her husband abandoned her with a four-year-old daughter and another child on the way. Kwan tells Olivia that all the water in her mother's belly "poured out as tears from her eyes. . . . That poor starving baby in her belly ate a hole in my mother's heart, and they both died" (14). In this way, years later, Olivia learns what Kwan has always known. Their father had no legal or hereditary claim to the name Jack Yee. The name belonged to the owner of a stolen overcoat that the young university student who became their father purloined from a drunken man who had been trying to sell it for whatever cash he could get. In the coat's pockets were immigration permits, academic records, notification of admission to an American university, a ticket for passage on a ship, and cash—documents that would facilitate a new life in a wealthy country full of opportunity, far away from poverty, factory work, a pregnant wife, and a child. Donning the coat and the spectacles he found in one pocket, and appropriating the documents, the student became Jack Yee. But Amy Tan does not privilege Kwan's version. Kwan, in fact, prefaces her tale by saying that she heard it from Li Bin-bin, her mother's sister who raised her—and who, under the circumstances, would be unlikely to feel kindly toward the bogus Jack Yee.

Thus the question remains: Who is the man behind the identity of Jack Yee? Kwan says that she has never known his true name, and she clearly knows almost nothing of his origins. And by extension, then, who are Olivia and Kwan? Who are their true ancestors? And who are Miss Banner and Nunumu? And, ultimately, how are all of these individuals connected?

Finally, Tan employs the many-layered triple narrative to interrogate the accounts of actual historical events, perhaps even to suggest that such accounts are unstable because they are the productions of gendered, class-defined, or racially constructed language. The Taiping Rebellion of the mid-nineteenth century is well known to Sinologists as well as to historians and geographers, but the standard texts tend toward factual, Westernized accounts of military battles, descriptions of territory gained or lost, and tallies of victories and defeats. Kwan's version of the Rebellion privileges the perspective of a half-blind orphan who notices far more than battles between Manchu and Hakka. For one-eyed Nunumu, the Rebellion means the loss of her entire family, and life in a half-deserted village populated only by the elderly and the very young, the physically and mentally disabled, and the cowardly; the Heavenly King and his armies succeed only in bringing her hunger and cold, and a life of servitude in a house full of missionaries. Nunumu's experiences factor the personal element into a historical equation, revealing the frequently overlooked truth that military and political battles are always won or lost at the expense of thousands of individuals whose lives are forever disrupted by the ambitions of a powerful minority and their followers.

NARRATIVE POINT OF VIEW

The Hundred Secret Senses has two narrators: Olivia and Kwan. Olivia, from whose point of view the novel is structured, provides the frame story—an autobiographical narrative about her California childhood, her marriage, and her relationship with her older half-sister who emigrated to the United States when Olivia was a small child. Within the context of Olivia's story, Kwan speaks about her own life, telling stories about her colorful past, giving shape to her personal histories, giving voice to events that connect people and relationships between centuries and continents.

As Olivia narrates her own story, she reveals that at the core of her identity lie angst and unhappiness, doubts and skepticism. In Olivia's version of events, life has been one long series of rejections—first by her father who "abandons" her by dying when she is only four years old, then by her mother whose energy is consumed by a succession of boy-friends, and finally by Simon who appears never to have come to terms with the loss of his first love. Having decided that she needs her mother's complete attention as well as Simon's undiluted love, and having finally, grudgingly, decided that she will probably receive neither, Olivia is blind to Kwan's genuine affection, failing to appreciate the gift of love that her half-sister wants to bestow on her. As an adult, Olivia is constantly plagued by guilt whenever she is irritated by Kwan's ebullient attentions, and she worries because she feels incapable of reciprocating Kwan's un-flagging loyalty.

Olivia's tendency to assume that she has been rejected influences not only her interpretation of the events of her life but also her assessment of Kwan's and Simon's places in her world. She is unable to accept Kwan's unconditional love or to believe that Simon genuinely loves her and not the ghost of the dead Elza. Olivia brushes off affectionate ges-tures from Kwan and Simon, or misreads their words and actions, won-dering suspiciously why they refuse to leave her life, armoring herself in a casual attitude that she believes makes her impervious to further rejection. Her stories are well-chosen and cleverly constructed, her re-marks intelligent, glib, witty, flip, but her insecurity colors her voice, making her sound occasionally petulant, frequently self-pitying, even maudlin.

The other major voice in the novel is Kwan's—a strong, memorable voice that is notable for its pragmatism as well as for its imagery. Al-though the novel is Olivia's story, Kwan gradually takes over with her distinctive talk story blend of travel narrative, legend, folktale, wry ob-servation, and misremembered or reconstructed history as she attempts to make Olivia understand and finally acknowledge that they have a history together that goes back over a century.

If Olivia is skeptical and full of self-doubt, Kwan has a voice that embodies faith and total confidence in the universe and in herself. She believes in the World of *Yin*, she believes in second chances, she believes television commercials, and she certainly believes in her own abilities. Kwan cheerfully takes people to task for risking their health, dispenses her own versions of herbal lore and remedies, and offers unsolicited advice on sundry aspects of life from mending shattered crockery to patching up broken relationships. In fact, Kwan is so perfectly sure of her fluency in English that she corrects her husband: "Not *stealed*. . . .

Stolened'' (21). She is equally certain about the soundness of the advice offered by her *yin* friends, and at one point she announces to the disbelieving Olivia that Lao Lu, a friend from the Taiping days and now a *yin* person, has decreed that Olivia and Simon must remain married because their fates are forever intertwined.

Kwan has two separate and distinctive voices. The voice in which she carries on her everyday conversations is an immigrant's, characterized by her use of the Chinese American patois to negotiate with verve and surety the daily transactions of her life. Her other voice, which has the cadences and rhythms of myth, legend, and folktale, transports Olivia—and the reader—into another world and another time. Through this fluent voice with its haunting images and sensory details, Kwan brings to life the story of the friendship between Nunumu and Miss Banner. Although Kwan's immigrant voice irritates Olivia, the poetic voice soothes, cajoles, resonates, and influences, leading Olivia to wonder, "So which part was her dream, which part was mine? Where did they intersect?" (29).

CHARACTER DEVELOPMENT

The Hundred Secret Senses is about the lives of two distinct groups of major characters from different centuries and different cultures. Dominating the novel through their position in the framing twentieth-century American narrative are Olivia, her half-sister Kwan, and her husband Simon, while in the nineteenth-century Chinese stories told by Kwan are Nunumu, Miss Banner, and Yiban. Scores of other characters populate the world of the novel, adding color, action, and variety.

In her late thirties, Olivia is a thoroughly contemporary Californian—Berkeley graduate, professional photographer, more yuppie than Chinese. With a Chinese father and a mother who describes herself as "American mixed grill, a bit of everything white, fatty, and fried" (3), Olivia seems overly conscious of her appearance, especially because she is sure that her name—Olivia Laguni—is completely at odds with her Asian features. Within her family, Olivia has always been compared with her Chinese father whose appearance and personality she is said to have inherited; an aunt frequently points out the fact that Olivia does not gain weight as her father did not, and her mother points out her tendency to be analytical, supposedly because she has her father's "accountant mentality" (20).

As a child, Olivia was embarrassed by Kwan, who on arrival in the United States was too different from anyone Olivia had ever encountered. Kwan was too Chinese, too alien, too un-American in her behavior. Now an adult, Olivia is still embarrassed by Kwan, but with the wisdom of maturity, she also feels guilty about her attitude. Uncomfortably, Olivia admits that over the years she has not been kind or accepting to Kwan, refusing as a little girl to play with her odd sister, yelling derisively at her, and telling lies to avoid spending much time with her. "I've done nothing to endear myself to her," says Olivia, baffled by Kwan's insistent loyalty.

After years of listening to Kwan's stories and trying not to credit them, Olivia publicly projects a skeptical persona although inwardly she continues to worry about whether Kwan might be right about the existence of *yin* people. Olivia still is uncomfortable when she recalls that as a child she was able to see Kwan's invisible friends, and she constantly searches for ways to prove that her early experiences were the result of a child's imagination run riot. "I was pretending," she wails when Kwan reminds her that she has not always been an unbeliever. "Ghosts come from the imagination, not the World of Yin" (142). Olivia's skepticism also is a function of her deeply felt conviction that she is unworthy of love. She believes that her mother and Simon have never loved her sufficiently. As a consequence, she finds it difficult to acknowledge Kwan's unconditional love or to accept Simon's genuine passion for her—and she conceals her doubts behind a bright skepticism tinged with suspicion.

Readers and critics have noted that Kwan is one of Amy Tan's most delightful and memorable character creations. On first meeting her new half-sister at the San Francisco Airport, Olivia gets the impression of a loud, extroverted, odd little person, short and chubby and badly dressed. That first image proves indelibly accurate; on further acquaintance, Kwan proves to be "a tiny dynamo . . . a miniature bull in a china shop" (20). Moreover, Kwan never quite understands the principles that supposedly govern Western fashion, and she embarrasses Olivia by appearing in public in an outfit of turquoise trousers paired with a purple checked jacket.

Completely enamored of the United States and her new family, Kwan sets out to experience her new life with huge enthusiasm. So indiscriminately does she embrace all things American that Olivia's brother Tommy remarks that Kwan "believes in free speech, free association, free car wash with fill-'er'-up" (20). Kwan's delight in her new siblings turns her into the family babysitter and surrogate mother, and Louise Laguni cheerfully relinquishes all responsibility to Kwan. Olivia's childhood memories all feature Kwan in the maternal roles that should have been played by Louise: when Olivia is taken ill at school, Kwan picks her up and brings her home; when Olivia weeps over some childhood disappointment, Kwan comforts her.

Kwan is a bit out of the ordinary in many ways, some of which defy explanation. She cannot come within three feet of a television without its hissing, and she has refused to wear a watch since the day she strapped on a digital watch and the numbers commenced to change rapidly like slot machine icons. After two hours, the watch stopped running permanently. Clearly, watches do not function properly on Kwan's wrist. Another peculiarity is the fact that without any electrical training, Kwan is able to pinpoint the source of a problem in an electrical circuit. In addition, she can reactivate a nonfunctioning cordless phone temporarily by pressing on the recharger nodes. Kwan clearly—and mysteriously— has a profound effect on things electrical and electronic, although she does nothing to precipitate appliances' strange reactions to her proximity.

Kwan's most distinctive characteristic is her regular conversations with people who are already dead. "I have yin eyes," she tells Olivia one night. "I can see yin people" (14). When Olivia sleepily demands an explanation, Kwan informs her that *yin* people are those who have already died. Although Kwan appears to have visitors from all sectors of the World of *Yin* and speaks with a multitude of *yin* people, her most talkative and opinionated contact from that invisible world is Lao Lu, who, like Kwan, lived with and worked for the missionaries who inhabited the Ghost Merchant's house in nineteenth-century Changmian. Kwan claims that her ability to converse with the *yin* people is the result of her highly developed "hundred secret senses," which she describes as similar to "ant feet, elephant trunk, dog nose, cat whisker, whale ear, bat wing, clam shell, snake tongue, little hair on flower" (102). She tells Olivia that the hundred secret senses resemble the other senses, other modes of knowing, other avenues from the outside world into the soul. These secret senses are the keys to Kwan's certitude about life; they are her connections to other lives.

Another of Kwan's unique traits is her determined persistence. Although the young Olivia has assiduously avoided learning to speak Chinese, Kwan insinuates language lessons into her nightly conversations with the child, telling fascinating stories in Chinese, with the result that

Olivia learns the language unconsciously and with little effort. "She pushed her Chinese secrets into my brain," Olivia recalls, adding that her worldview has been immeasurably altered by her association with Kwan (12). Years later, when Olivia and Simon initiate divorce proceedings, Kwan determinedly maneuvers them into traveling to China with her because she is convinced that their true destiny awaits them in that country. Olivia finds Kwan's persistence particularly trying, especially Kwan's dogged determination to be loyal to her no matter how she behaves toward Kwan; despite countless rebuffs, Kwan cheerily persists in remaining an important component of Olivia's life.

Olivia's husband, Simon Bishop, is a more sympathetic—and somewhat more fully developed—character than most of the male characters in Tan's other novels. Differing from the cardboard figures or nearly invisible men of *The Joy Luck Club*, men who tend to be patriarchal authority figures or male nonentities, or the brutal Wen Fu in *The Kitchen God's Wife*, Simon is more multifaceted, very much a product of the late twentieth century. He is a man who mourns the death of his first love, who argues with Olivia over custody of a Yorkshire terrier–Chihuahua mixed breed dog, and who is not too proud to accept a dinner invitation from Kwan if it is the only strategy that will allow him to remain connected with Olivia. Although he helped to write the proposal for the travel article about Chinese cuisine, he offers to give up the China trip if Olivia thinks that she might be more comfortable traveling with another writer. Unlike the men in other Tan novels, Simon is neither monster nor detached observer; he is, instead, a vulnerable man who seems puzzled and even hurt by Olivia's request for a divorce.

Like Olivia, Simon has a multiethnic background, which includes a Chinese ancestor; unlike Olivia, he is far less Chinese and more definitively Western. While Olivia grew up in and around Chinese communities, Simon spent his childhood in Utah. He, in fact, identifies himself as Hawaiian, although Kwan claims to see a resemblance between him and her sister, saying at one point that Olivia and Simon look like twins. Nevertheless, as attractive as he is, Simon remains far less interesting than the women characters, and, in fact, lacks even the vignette brilliance of minor characters like Zeng, the one-eared peddler; Rocky, the ambitious taxi driver in Guilin; or Du Lili, Kwan's elderly friend in Changmian.

Kwan's dream-like stories about her previous existence are focused on the linked lives of two women: Nunumu, the Hakka girl that Kwan claims is herself in a previous life, and Nelly Banner, the American woman to whom Nunumu gives her complete loyalty and, finally, her life. So vivid are Kwan's narratives, so compelling are the episodes that she recounts, that the novel becomes as much the story of Nunumu and Miss Banner as it is the story of Kwan and Olivia.

Nunumu occupies the center of Kwan's stories about life with the Jesus Worshippers. Orphaned in the mass enthusiasm for the Taiping cause, Nunumu is one-eyed, the result of a childhood injury from a falling rock, but she is courageous and resourceful. She eventually makes her way from her devastated home village to Jintian and then into the household of the missionaries where she works as a servant and as Miss Banner's companion. Nunumu teaches Miss Banner to speak Chinese and becomes her confidante, and after six years during which their friendship grows and strengthens, they flee together into the mountains in a vain attempt to escape the marauding Manchu soldiers.

Nelly Banner is a drifter. American by birth, she spent part of her childhood in India and Malacca, and after her father died, she lived with a succession of lovers before she found herself abandoned by the latest lover in Canton where she met the English missionaries and began traveling with them. When Nunumu saves Miss Banner from drowning, the two women's lives become entwined, and with her heroic act, Nunumu takes on the responsibility for Miss Banner's life and well-being. Kwan tells Olivia that because of the rescue, Nunumu's and Miss Banner's lives had "flowed together in that river, and became as tangled and twisted as a drowned woman's hair" (38).

Through the novel parades an astonishingly vivid collection of minor characters, none of them completely developed, but all of them distinctively rendered and memorable. The best of these fantastic figures inhabit Kwan's stories about Nunumu's life in the Ghost Merchant's house: pompous and deceitful General Cape with his military costumes; half-Chinese and half-American Yiban, driven by his devotion to Miss Banner; nervous Miss Mouse; fervent Pastor Amen; opium-eating Dr. Too Late. But no less attention-getting are some of the dramatis personae from Kwan's twentieth-century childhood: Buncake who never speaks but only waves her hands and carols "Lili lili" in a high voice; Du Yun who is so overcome with grief that she imagines she has become her dead adopted daughter; Third Auntie, the clairvoyant who explains to Li Bin-bin and Du Lili why Kwan and Buncake appear to have become one and the same little girl; and finally, the nameless young girls who struggle up a steep mountain to set birds free in return for wishes come true.

SETTING

Setting in *The Hundred Secret Senses* serves to highlight the geographical backgrounds and cultural realities of Kwan's life, as well as the rich dual heritage that Olivia and Simon share as American-born Chinese. Like Tan's two earlier books, the novel is set in America and China—two locations that are separated temporally and spatially, culturally and historically—but unlike those two novels, *Secret Senses* also attempts to identify connections and draw parallels between two centuries.

Olivia's San Francisco is a thoroughly American metropolis, a late-twentieth-century urban environment that embraces equally a motley assortment of inhabitants: free-lance artists and writers; the Market Street eccentric who loudly prophesies to passers-by that California will one day slide into the ocean "like a plate of clams" (19); people walking dogs on the trails of the Presidio; AIDS patients; women who regularly spend their time at spas; Chinese immigrants caught between the Old World and the New. Geographically, the novel's San Francisco encompasses Golden Gate Park (where Olivia and Simon are married in an outdoor ceremony), Chinatown and Balboa Street, the Sunset district, and Pacific Heights, on the fringes of which Olivia and Simon have purchased a co-op apartment in a renovated Victorian house. Although Kwan has been a San Francisco resident for over thirty years, the city has never become her natural landscape. She moves through the city and its neighborhoods with the ease of a long-time resident, sniffing out sales at "Emporium Capwell," chatting with long-time customers at the drugstore where she works, arguing with a veterinarian over a bill; but China remains her constant point of reference, and Olivia notices that Kwan has recently begun to mention China in nearly every conversation.

Half a world away from San Francisco, twentieth-century Changmian seems to be almost a Chinese Brigadoon, unchanged and picturesque despite the major political and ideological upheavals. Olivia's first glimpse of Changmian reveals to her a landscape straight out of a glossy travel poster, a scene that in reality has been photographed and displayed in glossy magazines countless times. She sees a rural community nestled at the base of two jagged karst peaks with vivid green forested flanks. The village itself consists of rows of whitewashed houses with tile roofs, and surrounding the houses are carefully tended fields and ponds bisected and intersected with stone walls and irrigation canals. Olivia immediately falls under the seductive spell of the village, feeling that she has discovered "a fabled misty land, half memory, half illusion" (205), and she realizes with surprise that Changmian is a familiar landscape, the setting for the stories that Kwan insinuated into her dreams time and again years before. Changmian is Kwan's emotional and psychological homeland, the native landscape of her lives, and the place to which she must finally return to fulfill her dreams. And despite her thirty-year absence and a full life in a completely different culture and landscape, Kwan slips unobtrusively, seamlessly back into the domestic routine at Big Ma's and Du Lili's house in the village.

Kwan's narratives also reveal another Changmian, a village that during the Taiping years is an impoverished enclave in a valley below rugged limestone mountains tunneled with hundreds of caves through which the wind blows incessantly. From the garden of the Ghost Merchant's house, Nunumu can see the village houses below as well as the stone archway that leads into the next valley, and further away, the mountains where she once roamed as a child; but her daily existence is now defined by the walls that enclose the house, its overgrown garden, and the pavilion where the previous owner is said to have died. For six years, Nunumu's circumscribed life within those walls reflects her position as a servant to the missionaries who inhabit the house and grounds. For five days each week, she washes and irons the missionaries' clothing, mends torn garments, cooks, and cleans. On Sundays, like all of the other servants and many of the village people, she is required to attend long worship services conducted by Pastor Amen. Only on Saturdays does Nunumu venture beyond the garden walls, and then only in the company of Miss Banner to distribute religious tracts to the inhabitants of Changmian.

Throughout the novel, Changmian displays two faces: one face presents the magical timeless village of Kwan's edited memories and Olivia's first impressions; the other face belongs to the poor but vibrant community that proudly—and joyously—sends its best and strongest citizens to fight for the cause of the Heavenly King in the Taiping wars, and a century later participates with equal enthusiasm in the frenzied rush to cash in on a significant archaeological discovery—the luminous underground lake and prehistoric village that come to light during the search for Kwan in the mountain caves. In all of its incarnations, Changmian is the setting for Kwan's epic narrative of love and loss and rebirth—and both Changmians become the sites of Olivia's journey toward self. The mythic, timeless village calls Olivia back from twentieth-century California to the ancient landscape that witnessed the flowering of love between Yiban and Miss Banner; but it is in the primitive village with mud streets and lively chattering people that Olivia begins the process of reconnection with her psyche and then with Simon.

LITERARY DEVICES

So adept is Amy Tan's handling of figurative language, so precise is her choice of words and her crafting of verbal pictures, that memorable characters and thematically significant settings come to life in the novel. Through her use of symbol clusters and images, Tan creates fictional stages on which her characters play their roles, enacting the conflicts through which Tan explores the power of memory and the nature of relationships.

Sometimes whimsical, other times evocative, occasionally surreal, chapter titles reiterate the novel's themes, foreshadowing and calling attention to the images and symbols that ornament the text. Images summoned by the titles serve to reinforce the sense of otherworldliness, the mystery of Kwan's stories: ''The Girl with the Yin Eyes,'' ''The Ghost Merchant's House,'' ''The Catcher of Ghosts,'' even ''When Light Balances with Dark.'' Other titles suggest temporality, important events and everyday occurrences, the passage of time: ''The Funeral,'' ''Hello Goodbye,'' ''Kwan's Fiftieth,'' ''The Year of No Flood''; still others prefigure the novel's food imagery: ''Kwan's Kitchen,'' ''The Best Time to Eat Duck Eggs,'' or ''Six-Roll Spring Chicken.''

Miss Banner's music box plays a significant role in the Changmian years and thus in Kwan's stories, as well as later, in Olivia's experiences. The box, a gift to Miss Banner from her father, is a safe hiding place for her diary and assorted keepsakes. During worship services, the missionaries use the box to accompany their singing although they have had to write new words to accompany the tune, which is inappropriate because it is a German drinking song. When Miss Banner attempts to elope with General Cape, Nunumu buries the box, symbolically obliterating all memories of her friend who has—Nunumu feels—betrayed their friendship. After Miss Banner returns and falls in love with Yiban, Nunumu unearths the box and restores it to its owner. Months later, with the missionaries dead and the clear threat of danger surrounding the Ghost Merchant's house, Miss Banner and Nunumu carefully pack the music box with mementos and reminders of their dead companions—a pill bottle, a glove, a button, a travel book, a tin of special tea. They light candles, turn the key to play the music box, and listen to the tinkling notes of the familiar melody—and in that way, they perform a homely funeral service for their dead friends. When the comforting ritual is over, they flee, carrying the box, to the cave in the mountains where Nunumu has left Yiban waiting for Miss Banner.

In those very mountains a century later, Olivia watches as Kwan pries open a reddish wooden box trimmed in brass. When she lifts the lid, the lilting high-pitched sounds of a martial melody emanate from the box, and Kwan removes from the box a kidskin glove, a small book—*A Visit to India, China, and Japan*—with deckled edges, a small tin, a journal with notes about unfamiliar food and snippets of information about the Taiping followers. The journal is dated 1859, and Olivia remembers Kwan's bedtime stories about a year identified as *Yi ba liu si*, the Chinese words for 1864. Kwan's Nunumu stories are set in 1864, just five years after the journal's date, and Olivia realizes that it is just possible for Miss Banner to have owned the volume. Struggling with her need for logical explanations, Olivia is forced to ask herself some crucial questions about Kwan's stories, especially about the reasons why Kwan has been so insistent that Olivia listen attentively to those stories—and at that moment, on that mountain, Olivia experiences an epiphany. She realizes that she has always known somehow, instinctively, why Kwan persists in telling story after story about Nunumu and Miss Banner; however, Olivia has resisted acknowledging her awareness of Kwan's reasons. Over the years, Kwan has asked, "Libby-ah, you remember?" And Olivia has denied, both to herself and to Kwan, any memory, knowing as she disclaims all knowledge of the past, that Kwan is hoping to hear her say, "of course I remember. I was Miss Banner"(321). As Olivia and Kwan turn over the tangible evidence of the truth of Kwan's stories about the Ghost Merchant's house, Olivia realizes that she can no longer deny that she and Kwan might indeed have had a shared history that began a century before Kwan's arrival at the San Francisco airport.

The major symbol group in the novel involves food in all its guises, its preparation, its consumption, its significance. Food becomes a literary language; gastronomic images and motifs provide Kwan with the means of re-creating her life as Nunumu in the last days of the Taiping regime, as well as with the words to re-create the story of Buncake, the little girl whose body Kwan appropriated long ago after the floods. Food also functions as a symbol for the intensity of the culture shock that Olivia and Simon experience when they travel to China with Kwan. And in the end, food for Olivia comes to represent Kwan's nurturing presence—and Olivia's own salvation.

Attempting to nudge Olivia into overcoming her skepticism and traveling with her into the memory of their life together in the Ghost Merchant's house, Kwan conjures up vivid recollections of the food and meals that she remembers from that existence. She contrasts the lavish Western breakfasts consumed by the missionaries during the peaceful years of plenty, with the sparse scavenged dinners that mark the years of starvation during the conflict between Manchu and Taiping. Bacon and eggs, corn cakes and fruit give way to fried locusts and grasshoppers, frogs and bats, that Nunumu and Lao Lu identify for the missionaries as "rabbit" so as not to disgust the squeamish Western palates. But although food imagery can be a powerful aid to the recovery of buried memories, Kwan's recollections of these distinctive meals do not evoke any answering reminiscences from Olivia, who listens politely and even interestedly, but disclaims any memory of the meals that Kwan is describing in such detail.

One especially notable food motif is preserved duck eggs, which for Kwan symbolize Nunumu's subversive resourcefulness. Because she loves duck eggs so much, Nunumu steals eggs—one or two at a time—from the missionaries, although she is careful to point out that they prefer chicken eggs to duck eggs. Nunumu preserves the eggs in quantities of precious salt to which she has free access because she supposedly needs the salt for removing stains from the weekly laundry. She coats the salted eggs in mud, and stores them in cracked pottery jars for which she barters some of her precious eggs. The preserved duck eggs represent security for Nunumu, who eventually squirrels away ten rows of jars full of eggs, and the eggs become the missionaries' sustenance when food supplies run short during the Manchu wars with the Taiping kingdom. The eggs also create the opportunity for Nunumu to experience her own romance when Zeng, the peddler who supplies her with jars in exchange for eggs, decides that he wants her to become his wife. For Nunumu, the first hint of Zeng's courtship surfaces when he offers to give her an unblemished jar even when she has no eggs to trade because the missionaries have eaten most of them.

Amy Tan also uses food imagery as a characterization device. When Kwan recounts the story of Buncake, Kwan's description of Du Yun's skillful preparation of fried frogs provides a painful parallel to Buncake's recollections of how her mother and father died. Buncake, who has been orphaned by the early "re-education" efforts that swept China just before the total communist take-over, is taken in by Kwan's aunt, Du Yun, a woman who prides herself on one special culinary creation—freshly killed frogs, quickly sauteed in hot oil until they are crisp. As Du Yun deftly skins and dismembers the frogs, she fails to notice that Buncake is cowering silently behind Kwan with her fist jammed into her mouth "like a sandbag stopping a leak in a riverbank" (250). Speechless, Buncake is unable to explain to Du Yun that the scene is horrifically distressing, that "this tearing of skin from flesh" reminds her of how her mother and father had died while she watched from the tree in which her father had hidden her. Buncake has not spoken since then because her last promise to her mother had been that she would be quiet and not say a word or make a sound.

For Olivia and Simon, food symbolizes the profound dislocation that they experience in China. The trip is originally conceived as a journalistic odyssey during which they would work on a free-lance project for a travel and food magazine. "We would offer to write and photograph a story on village cuisine of China," recalls Olivia, adding that their grand dreams included other similar articles, a book and lecture tour, even a TV series. When they finally are persuaded to accompany Kwan to China, Olivia and Simon envision taking exotic photographs and writing evocative text, and they arrive in Guilin ready to avail themselves of every possible photo opportunity. At first, they are not disappointed; they breakfast on freshly cooked pancakes from a street vendor as they stroll past colorful displays of fruit and other produce, as well as a variety of other wares for sale. As Olivia focuses a photograph of a bustling street market, Simon makes notes for the accompanying text and scouts around the stalls for other photographic possibilities. At the bird market, Olivia is fascinated by a beautiful white owl with eyes that remind her of chocolate. Sensing her interest, the seller offers Olivia and Simon the owl with the suggestion that they take it to a nearby restaurant to be butchered and cooked for their evening meal. The two are, predictably, disturbed. Protesting when Kwan begins a spirited round of haggling with the bird seller, and visibly upset when Kwan purchases the owl, Olivia is not appeased until she discovers that Kwan's intent is to climb a mountain and release the owl so that it can fly from a mountaintop carrying Kwan's wishes. What Olivia does not yet know is that the true test of their capacity to stomach the strange and the unfamiliar awaits them in Changmian at the home where Kwan grew up.

Fascinated by Olivia's camera, Kwan's family friend, Du Lili, goes out of her way to stage interesting photographic subjects, at one point slashing a chicken's neck and then letting the bird stumble around on the ground until it falls dead. As she dismembers the chicken and then cooks it in its own blood, she chatters about how she has intentionally prolonged the butchering to give Olivia a more interesting subject to photograph. Appalled, Olivia worries about dinner, having finally confronted the tremendous difference between her expectations about China and the realities with which she is confronted. After watching Du Lili, Olivia finds the chicken stew unappetizing at best, but she also knows that there is nothing else that she can eat, "no ham and cheese in the fridge—there's no fridge!" (266). Because they are hungry, she and Simon tentatively try the chicken, and to their surprise, they find the stew flavorful. Before the evening is over, they also have imbibed "pickle-mouse wine," which displays at the bottom of the wine bottle a grayish object with a tail. The old Olivia of just a week earlier would have been sickened at the idea of drinking any liquid in which a mouse has been preserved—in fact, she is silently wondering why she does not feel the need to vomit. Instead, she and Simon burst out in uncontrollable laughter, apprehension giving way to catharsis, possibly because at that point they understand that this meal has been their gastronomic initiation—and they have not only survived but triumphed over their inhibitions and preconceptions. They have progressed far beyond their initial idea of superficial travelogue articles with glossy photographs to an authentic home-cooked Chinese meal in a genuine Chinese village. Moreover, they have thoroughly enjoyed the experience and are suffused with feelings of well-being.

Food for Kwan is a form of nurturing communication, the language of love and acceptance through which she continues her efforts to bond with Olivia. When she finds twelve-year-old Olivia weeping, Kwan immediately assumes that little Olivia has consumed more than her share of the Christmas cookies that Kwan has baked and is suffering from a stomachache. To Kwan, the solution is simple—she will decrease the sugar in the next batch of cookies so that Olivia can eat as many as she wants. Worrying years later about Olivia who looks unhappy and exhausted in the weeks following her separation from Simon, Kwan invites her to dinner, promising that the menu will include Olivia's favorite dish, potstickers, and indicating that a supply of wontons will be available for Olivia's freezer. For another dinner, Kwan offers Olivia dried scallops, a rare and precious delicacy that costs an astonishing sixty dollars per pound. Unfortunately, despite her enjoyment of Kwan's excellent cooking, Olivia repeatedly fails to decode the messages of love and sisterly concern that Kwan conveys through her offerings of food.

At the end of the novel, food becomes Olivia's salvation, revealing to her in rather dramatic fashion the unbreakable connections between the past and the present. Standing in a drizzle with the small group of mourners at Big Ma's grave, Olivia watches as Du Lili places a preserved duck egg into Big Ma's hand before the coffin is lowered into the ground. The sight of the egg awakens in Olivia the memory of Nunumu's cache of preserved duck eggs, and before she is completely aware of what she is doing, she races to the ruins of the Ghost Merchant's house and begins to dig frantically near where she thinks the old garden wall might once have stood. Her efforts soon reveal a pottery jar that she immediately breaks open with the handle of her hoe. From that jar, she extracts one age-darkened egg after another, cradling the fragile muddy eggs to her chest against which they crumble and disintegrate. For Olivia, the eggs are "relics of [her] past disintegrating into gray chalk," but she is unperturbed at the loss of the eggs: "I knew I had already tasted what was left" (355). If Olivia has needed any further evidence to support Kwan's reminiscences, she has that evidence lying before her in the muddy trench that she has dug in the Ghost Merchant's garden: the eggs are the final corroboration that Kwan's stories are records of real events and real individuals; each crumbling egg is the ultimate proof of connections and resonances between one life and the next, between one continent and another one on the other side of the globe.

CULTURAL AND HISTORICAL CONTEXTS

A fairly substantial portion of *The Hundred Secret Senses* is set in nineteenth-century China—more specifically in the 1850s and 1860s during the Taiping Rebellion, the most important peasant-led revolt in Chinese history. The Taiping regime, led by the charismatic Hong Xiuquan, gained strength during the Qing Dynasty in the wake of the opium wars, the opening of China's borders to foreign trade, and the loss of Hong Kong to the British crown. At its height, the rebellion involved over 600,000 men and 500,000 women. Borrowing their ideology and teachings from Christianity, the Taiping followers rebelled against what they considered to be corruption and obsolescence in the imperial court, demanding widespread changes that included equality for women, agricultural reform, and the abolition of private property.

Educated in part by Western missionaries whose teachings apparently resonated with his own naturally mystical leanings, Hong Xiuquan converted to Christianity, and thereafter claimed not only that he was Jesus Christ's younger brother, but also that his relationship to Jesus made him the Heavenly King on earth. He recruited thousands of followers from the peasant classes by announcing his intention to create *Taiping tianguo*, or "a Heavenly Kingdom of Great Peace" in which the faithful would labor together for the good of the community. In this kingdom, everyone would have equal access to education, and footbinding and slavery would be outlawed. In addition, undesirable habits such as gambling, drinking alcohol, and smoking tobacco would be forbidden.

The Heavenly Kingdom flourished until 1864 in Nanjing, which had become its capital. During that summer, two provincial armies, financed by a coalition of the French, the British, and the Qing government, marched into Nanjing. When he realized that he could not defend his "kingdom" against the superior might of the massed European and Chinese forces, Hong Xiuquan committed suicide. Rather than surrendering, his men followed suit. A few weeks later, Nanjing fell to the invading armies, and the Heavenly Kingdom ceased to exist.

Amy Tan has chosen to identify Nunumu/Kwan with a distinctive minority ethnic Chinese group whose name, Hakka, which means "foreigner," was originally a pejorative label for the ethnic peoples who migrated from northern China to settle in the southern provinces. Because Hong Xiuquan was of Hakka origin, and also because the Taiping regime advocated equality for women and banned foot-binding and prostitution, Nunumu and her people—the Hakka—are attracted to the teachings of the Heavenly King and are eager to join the rebellion. Like the Taiping rebels, the Hakka were known for their egalitarian leanings, and Hakka women—famed for their industry, cleverness, and physical strength—never bound their feet, even during the Qing period when that custom was followed most rigidly. The independent Hakka found it difficult to gain acceptance from the peoples through whose lands they traveled. Speaking of her past life as Nunumu, Kwan says, "We were . . . Guest People—hnh!—meaning guests not invited to stay in any good place too long" (30). Because Nunumu is a one-eyed Hakka girl, she is an outsider. She has marginal status in China because of her ethnic heritage, in the Ghost Merchant's house because she is a Chinese servant in a household of Westerners, in the population at large because she is physically deformed. In San Francisco, Kwan is likewise marginal. Bob Laguni does not adopt her as he does Louise's children; consequently,

Kwan never legally becomes a part of the family. And finally, despite decades of life in California, Kwan still has not truly assimilated into middle American culture. She retains her Chinese-English speech, continues to live in a Chinatown neighborhood, persists in dressing like an immigrant, and still dreams of one day returning to China.

THEMES AND MAJOR ISSUES

Like Amy Tan's first two novels, *The Hundred Secret Senses* explores a number of issues that have become familiar to Tan's readers: family relationships—especially connections between generations, and the bonds between sisters; linguistic differences and miscommunication; identity; biculturalism, ethnicity, and the tensions of living between worlds; cultural dislocation; and women's roles. In this third novel, several new themes appear, among them love (in all its guises), loyalty, faith, and the unreliability of memory. Tan herself claims that the novel is about love, saying that *The Hundred Secret Senses* answers "a question about love, unconditional love" (Giles). While authorial intent and reader reaction are not always congruent, it is abundantly clear that love is a dominant theme in the novel.

Several forms of love are enacted throughout the novel: Louise Laguni's numerous infatuations; General Cape's mercenary courtship of a Chinese banker's daughter as well as his lustful pursuit of Miss Banner; the steady affection between Kwan and George (and Nunumu and Zeng); Miss Mouse's unrequited adoration of Dr. Too Late. Meanwhile, at the center of the novel are Olivia and Simon, soulmates by Kwan's (and Lao Lu's) definition despite the couple's impending divorce. In Kwan's universe, Olivia and Simon are simply continuing a great romance that began in the waning months of the Taiping when they were Miss Banner and Yiban Johnson. Complicating the central romance, however, is Olivia's belief that Simon still loves Elza who died before he met Olivia, and Simon's apparent inability to accept the finality of Elza's death suggests briefly the possibility of an obsessive love. Through the turmoil of the relationship between Olivia and Simon, Amy Tan examines love and its resilience, its capacity for enduring even beyond the ultimate separation, death; and she portrays the lengths to which human beings will go in search of love.

Tan also portrays another form of love that is as binding and enduring as romantic love—the love that forges unbreakable links between friends. This form of love, which is an intense combination of affection, respect, loyalty, and companionship, finds its clearest manifestation in the friendship between Nunumu and Miss Banner, and later in the unselfish sisterly love that Kwan offers to Olivia. During the trip to China, Kwan describes this kind of love as she remembers a fervent wish that she made before she left for America: "My first wish: to have a sister I could love with all my heart, only that, and I would ask for nothing more from her" (195). When her wish for a sister is granted, Kwan enthusiastically keeps her promise; her affection for Olivia is boundless and requires no reciprocity.

Another theme that surfaces in *The Hundred Secret Senses* involves loyalty and its opposite, betrayal. Kwan embodies loyalty; in fact she uses the word "loyalty" frequently in her everyday conversation as well as in her stories. In Kwan's tales, the loyalty of Nunumu to Miss Banner is so intense that the former leaves the safety of her mountain hiding place to lead Miss Banner to safety, and when it becomes clear that the approaching soldiers will overtake them, Nunumu stays with Miss Banner and dies with her. Despite his betrayal of her, Nelly Banner remains loyal to General Cape until events force her to understand that he is using her to gain access to the missionaries' funds and food supplies. And Zeng, whose courtship of Nunumu is so prosaic as to seem offhanded, proves his loyalty to her by returning immediately after he is killed by the Manchu to lead Nunumu and Yiban to the safety of the mountain caves. Zeng then vanishes immediately after promising that he will wait for Nunumu forever. Kwan herself is so loyal to her sister that Olivia's mean jokes in childhood and snide remarks as an adult have not deflected Kwan's love. On the contrary, each time Olivia rebuffs her efforts, Kwan simply tries harder and more often to be of use, to be supportive, to be helpful, and above all, to love.

As a contrast to Kwan's (and Nunumu's) loyalty, Amy Tan has created the character of the villainous General Cape who personifies treachery and betrayal. Telling one of her stories, Kwan recalls, "General Cape, he was rotten too. He threw away other people" (146). Cape abandons Miss Banner to marry the daughter of a wealthy banker, and when he is forced to flee after cuckolding the banker with the man's younger wives, Cape comes to Changmian to resume his affair with Miss Banner whose misplaced loyalty to him leads her to take him back. After staying with Miss Banner and the missionaries for two months, Cape disappears with the group's food supplies, pack animals, and mission money. When he reappears, he leads a gang of Manchu soldiers who lay waste to the countryside around Changmian. Cape and his men take over the Ghost Merchant's house, and when Lao Lu protests, they kill him.

The novel illustrates other and less dramatic forms of betrayal. At her husband's deathbed, Olivia's mother Louise vows never to remarry, and to spend the rest of her life honoring the name of Yee and the Chinese heritage that it represents. Yet within a short time, she has met and married Bob Laguni, and is raising completely assimilated American children who know next to nothing about Chinese culture. When she is a child, Olivia betrays Kwan by telling their parents that Kwan communicates with ghosts, and the alarmed parents promptly incarcerate Kwan in a mental hospital. As an adult, Olivia unthinkingly continues her betrayal of Kwan in small ways: pretending to be so busy that she cannot find the time to accept Kwan's invitations to dinner, giving Kwan only a token gift of an inexpensive faux tortoise-shell box at her big fiftieth-birthday celebration, never telephoning Kwan until the laundry basket is full and Olivia needs to use Kwan's washing machine. Despite these daily betrayals, Kwan loyally continues to refer to Olivia as her favorite sister, and Olivia continues to be overcome with guilt each time Kwan invites her to dinner, presents her with pre-cooked dinners for her freezer, or even telephones her.

In *The Hundred Secret Senses*, Amy Tan explores the theme of sisterhood—a departure from her earlier focus on mothers and daughters in her first two novels. Sisters are prominently featured in myth, folktale, and literature, frequently as rivals or antagonists, often as women estranged by birth order or parental favor. Cinderella and her ugly sisters, as well as King Lear's feuding daughters, are familiar examples of competition and conflict between sisters. Less generally familiar are Lizzie and Laura of Christina Rossetti's poem "Goblin Market"—sisters whose radically divergent attitudes toward life and experience separate them and threaten harm to Laura, until Lizzie's love for her sister leads her to risk death to save Laura. Unlike these traditional and literary treatments of sisterhood, Amy Tan chooses to focus on the ways in which sisters influence each other as they each work through the complicated process of defining a clear sense of self and a balanced identity.

In her study, *Psyche's Sisters: Re-Imagining the Meaning of Sisterhood*, Christine Downing points out that "the interactions among sisters . . . instigate the heroine's journey toward self, toward psyche." She continues, "Our sisterly relationships challenge and nurture us, even as we sometimes disappoint and betray one another" (3–4). *The Hundred Secret Senses* is primarily about Olivia's journey toward self and wholeness, and about the role that Kwan plays in Olivia's quest. From the time of her adored father's death when she was four years old, Olivia has felt unanchored, a feeling that has persisted into her adulthood, complicating every relationship she has had and rendering her incapable of freely accepting love. In the midst of Olivia's uncertainty, Kwan is the constant; Kwan, in fact, provides Olivia with a continuing long-lasting and stable human connection, although Olivia has never recognized the importance of Kwan's role in her life.

Before Kwan comes to San Francisco, Olivia at first mistakenly believes that she will be replaced when the new daughter arrives. Thus on hearing that Kwan will be an addition to the family rather than a replacement, Olivia is delighted, until she realizes that she will more than likely have to share her mother's limited time with the newcomer. Already feeling neglected by her mother, Olivia is in no mood to be forced into competition for attention. But not until Kwan is installed in the Laguni household does a worse possibility become obvious to Olivia: with Kwan in residence to look after the younger children, Louise Laguni has more time than ever to spend with her friends. As a consequence, Olivia has resented Kwan from the beginning for taking the place of the mother whose attention Olivia wanted desperately; and although Kwan capably performs the maternal role that Louise has abandoned, Olivia refuses to accept the substitution, rejecting Kwan's care and nurturance, and repudiating everything that Kwan represents.

The presence of Kwan in Olivia's life problematizes Olivia's relationship with and position in a cultural group to which she belongs by heritage—Asian Americans. For Olivia, Kwan represents ethnicity, a diaspora culture, and racial origins that comprise the visible half of Olivia's genetic inheritance and almost nothing of her cultural bias. Kwan is indelibly Other—she speaks with an accent and an incomplete command of English vocabulary, she wears odd clothes that mark her as an immigrant, and she claims regular communication with invisible correspondents from an insubstantial existence. By contrast, Olivia is all-American except for her Asian features; she dresses fashionably, and she is rational to a fault and skeptical as well. And yet, Kwan and Olivia are sisters; they share a father, and Kwan has been an important part of Olivia's life since the latter was a child.

Early in their relationship, young Olivia wants nothing to do with Chinese culture, which she equates with her strange new immigrant sister. She is embarrassed by her kinship with Kwan, playing cruel jokes on her that highlight their differences, and disclaiming any blood ties when neighborhood children taunt Kwan. As Olivia matures, her embarrassment gives way to guilt about her treatment of Kwan, and that guilt becomes a barrier to the development of any form of genuine companionship between the sisters. Yet despite Olivia's resistance and the unacknowledged gulf between them, Kwan has been responsible all along for anchoring Olivia in a community—although Olivia remains oblivious for years to the importance of the cultural context that she has acquired through her sister's insistent tutelage. Thanks to Kwan, Olivia speaks Chinese, knows late nineteenth-century Chinese history, and even identifies a Chinese dish as her favorite food. And when Olivia finally visits China and Kwan's native village for the first time, she is overwhelmed by the feeling that she has come home; and for the first time, she begins to feel her kinship with Kwan and to move toward integrating the elements of her heritage into a complete identity that includes the existence of a Chinese half-sister.

Like Olivia, Kwan needs sisterly help as she works to restore the harmony that has been absent from her life since she was Nunumu and told the lie that separated Yiban and Miss Banner. On one level, Kwan's stories about Nunumu and Miss Banner reflect her wistful hope that she and Olivia can forge strong ties of affection. The strength and persistence of her hopes become evident during the China journey when she remembers that as a young girl in Changmian, her greatest wish was to have a sister to love more than anyone else in the world. She admits having made a vow that if the wish were to come true, she would be perfectly content, never again wishing for anything else. On another level, Kwan's stories are prompts or hints that she hopes will remind Olivia of their common history; for only when Olivia is able to acknowledge their century-old connection will Kwan be able to absolve herself of her guilt.

In China, Olivia and Kwan are together again as they were when Olivia was a child, as they have not been in almost thirty years. In the geography that has shaped their lives, they re-establish their emotional connections with each other and they reaffirm a relationship that has endured through at least two lifetimes. More importantly, they are blessed with a rare opportunity: they are empowered to correct the mistakes of an earlier time, and as they rewrite their story, each one finds what she has been seeking—an integrated self for Olivia and peace for Kwan.

ALTERNATIVE READING: JUNGIAN
ARCHETYPAL CRITICISM

Advocates of archetypal criticism, sometimes called myth criticism, theorize the existence of what Gilbert Murray has described as "the memory of the race, stamped, as it were, upon our physical organism" (238–39). This racial memory—the residue of some form of universal human experience—is manifested in and through archetypes, or narrative patterns, symbols, images, themes, and character types that recur in literature, art, religion, folklore, ritual, and particularly in myths and dreams. An archetypal critic examines the appearance of these universal patterns and symbols in a literary text, studying their contextual implications, and seeking to formulate conclusions about the functions of those archetypes in the work.

Archetypal criticism had its earliest beginnings in the results of field-work in primitive cultures done by British anthropologist, Sir James George Frazer (1854–1941) whose research into ritual and magic among primitive peoples suggested to him the existence of recurrent narrative and ritual patterns common to widely dispersed cultures and societies. In his immense and influential comparison of mythologies, *The Golden Bough* (1890–1915), Frazer analyzes the parallels between the ritualistic patterns he had detected in primitive cultures and certain structural elements in myths, legends, and folktales. Although Frazer's work was eventually superseded—even disputed—by the work of later generations of anthropologists, his identification and documentation of seemingly universal patterns influenced some early twentieth-century literary critics, among them Gilbert Murray.

Even more important to the development of archetypal criticism is the work of Carl Gustav Jung, the Swiss psychiatrist and the founder of analytical psychology, who coined the term *collective unconscious* to describe the primordial and universal images that, according to Jung, have existed in the human imagination since the beginning of time. The images that make up the collective unconscious, the universal patterns and motifs that form the residue of an inborn shared human past, are called *archetypes*. Unable to discover a way to account for the recurrent images and patterns that appear in the narratives of disparate cultures, Jung suggests that archetypes, which are manifested through dreams, rituals, myths, religious beliefs, and literature, were shaped during the earliest periods of human existence. He further proposes that creative and imaginative expression derives its basic structures from natural occurrences—among them the cycle of birth and death and rebirth, the passage of seasons—or universal narrative patterns such as the *quest* or the *descent* to the *underworld*.

Archetypal critics differ in their critical methodologies, some drawing their strategies from a variety of disciplines—anthropology, history, psychology—and others relying solely on evidence from literary texts. But they do share certain core assumptions and purposes: that archetypes and archetypal patterns are universal, although they are manifested differently from culture to culture; and that the collective unconscious and its companion archetypes are the essential keys to the meaning of myth and ritual, dream and fantasy, narrative and—in the case of Amy Tan's fiction—talk story and feminine autobiography.

The Hundred Secret Senses lends itself particularly well to an archetypal analysis. To begin with, the novel contains several textual markers—narrative patterns or characters—strongly suggesting that an archetypal reading might yield valuable observations and insights. Early in the novel, Miss Banner's first attempts to speak about her life in Chinese suggest a world that defies logical comprehension—a plane of existence that normalizes little boys falling through a hole to the other side of the world, a school full of little Jesuses, money that smells like flowers and makes people happy. The description of a rationally impossible, shape-shifting world points to an archetypal universe or the dream landscape that often signals a journey into the unconscious where archetypes give shape to unarticulated thoughts. Another marker is the presence of characters who represent particular archetypes. One of these archetypal characters is Lao Lu, a *yin* person, a ghostly visitor from another existence who represents the Spirit archetype, and whose presence is a clear indicator of the tension between the novel's two worlds and the characters' multiple existences. Kwan has unfinished business from a previous life, and Lao Lu functions as her chief advisor in her efforts to complete her mission. Another archetypal figure is Big Ma whose name is a variant form of the title, "Great Mother," and who, in fact, has represented in Kwan's life the contradictory qualities of nurturance and destruction that are ascribed to the Great Mother archetype. After the death of Kwan's mother, Big Ma gave the orphaned child a home and raised her, but Kwan has always felt ambivalent about the older woman. Acknowledging Big Ma's largesse, Kwan nevertheless continues to resent the frequent slaps she endured as a child. In addition, Kwan is still bitter that Big Ma cheerfully shipped her off to America. Consequently, second only to

Kwan's desire to bring Olivia and Simon back together is her need to show Big Ma that the rejected orphan has become a successful American who can afford to visit her home village bearing heaps of gifts.

Still another archetypal marker is Tan's focus on the Changmian caves. In myth and folktale, caves are privileged as significant archetypal locations, denoting primal origins, birth, and rebirth. Before Olivia and Kwan can create a satisfactory conclusion for their shared story that began a century earlier, they must travel to the caves that represent the traumatic separations of that earlier existence: en route to the caves, Nunumu sees Zeng's shadow for the last time; in those caves, Yiban faces the knowledge that he will never see Nelly Banner again; and beside those caves, Nunumu and Miss Banner are killed by the Manchu soldiers. In addition to these markers, Kwan's dream-like narratives as well as Olivia's frequent references to dreams strongly indicate an examination that derives some of its methodology and critical apparatus from dream theory, which is a significant component of archetypal criticism. One might, in fact, read *The Hundred Secret Senses* as an extended archetypal dream through which Olivia attempts to sort out the psychological confusions and uncertainties as well as the emotional chaos of her life.

Early in the novel, Olivia introduces the dream motif, saying, "Because of Kwan, I have a talent for remembering dreams" (28), and then adding that throughout her childhood years, she believed that everyone remembered dreams as though they were other lives or even other identities. After years of drowsy listening as Kwan told stories at bedtime, and years of falling asleep while Kwan droned on at length about Changmian and *yin* people and Miss Banner, Olivia can no longer identify the boundaries between her own dreams and episodes in Kwan's stories. She is unable to recall those critical points at which her dream life seamlessly incorporated Kwan's voice spinning out events, people, and landscapes. For Olivia, dreams and stories are each part of the fabric of the other; stories are the verbal records of dreams, dreams are where the stories take shape.

The archetypal pattern that dominates *The Hundred Secret Senses* and structures the plot is the cycle of birth and death and rebirth, a pattern that is mirrored by the constant renewal in the natural world as winter gives way to spring and then summer, or the wet season succumbs to the dry months, year after year, century after century. Jungian psychologists have pointed out that the collective unconscious refuses to recognize finality, preferring instead to privilege cyclical change and renewal:

> In our dreams, as in our myths, death may figure not as the
> end, but as part of an overall process of growth and transfor-
> mation. Just as life is born from death in the material world
> . . . so our psychological and spiritual energies constantly re-
> create themselves, assuming new forms in our imagination.
> (Fontana 88)

Throughout the novel, birth and death are juxtaposed, linked in ways that suggest the clear relationship between the two events in Kwan's stories as well as in the grand cycle of the universe. As a result of Jack Yee's death, Kwan is "born" into the Laguni family to become Olivia's loyal sister and friend, as well as her guide to a previous life. Years before that, Buncake must die so that Kwan can return to life, "reborn" in her friend's body—again, so that eventually she can become a part of Olivia's life. And a century earlier, before Kwan's story begins, Yiban Johnson, born immediately after his mother's suicide by hanging, grows to manhood and falls in love with Nelly Banner, only to lose her because Nunumu fails to realize how well Yiban can deduce Miss Banner's thoughts. That mistake so haunts Nunumu that her primary mission in life after she becomes Kwan is to put things right by reuniting Nelly and Yiban, who are now Olivia and Simon.

Death is a pervasive motif in *The Hundred Secret Senses*, which begins when Olivia's father dies, and ends with Big Ma's funeral and the suggestion that Kwan is dead. With the exception of Jack Yee's death from illness, the deaths in the novel are unusual, even slightly surreal, creating the ambiance of a nightmare world and underscoring the dreamlike tone of the novel. Elza dies in an avalanche that overwhelms her as she angrily skis away from Simon to whom she has just announced that she is pregnant. Big Ma is so overjoyed at Kwan's impending visit to her village that she cannot wait, and hops aboard a minibus to surprise Kwan in Guilin. En route, the bus crashes, killing Big Ma on the very day that she should have been reunited with Kwan. Years earlier, Buncake drowns while she and Kwan are ensconced in a ditch that is so dry that they are pretending to be sitting in a boat. A sudden squall produces flash floods that overwhelm the two children who drown before they can scramble to safety. Kwan's tales about Changmian in the nineteenth century include several unusual demises. When Lao Lu makes an obscene remark about General Cape and Miss Banner, a soldier (possibly Cape?) beheads him. In a bizarre scene reminiscent of mass suicides within religious cults, the missionaries end their lives rather than face torture by the Manchu soldiers. After eating stale Communion bread and drinking water that they pretend is wine, Dr. Too Late, Miss Mouse, and Pastor and Mrs. Amen pray, then together they ingest all of the pills that remain in Dr. Too Late's medicine bag. Finally, Nunumu and Miss Banner die together, just a short distance from the safety of the caves somewhere on a mountain near Changmian, possibly hanged, although Kwan discounts that possibility because she says that hanging is too much trouble to arrange in a place with no trees.

Dreams of death, whether one's own or another's, can have several interpretations. Such dreams often suggest that the dreamer is grappling with deep-seated concerns, frequently including fear of loss of self or identity, dread of retribution for some fault or sin, and fear of alienation of affection. All of these fears are personified in Olivia. Even as an adult who appears to be comfortably assimilated into American culture, Olivia is plagued with questions and doubts about her Chinese ancestry, and she steadfastly continues to resist any suggestion that she and Kwan might have far more in common than a shared father. A problematic ethnicity is not the only source of Olivia's self-doubt. For over a decade and a half, she has identified herself primarily in relation to Simon, but throughout their marriage she has been unable to let go of her belief that Simon's affection for her is inconsequential compared to the love he still feels for the long-dead Elza. Olivia is certain that for Simon she is only second-best. Coupled with her insecurities in her marriage is Olivia's recurrent guilt about her inability to accept wholeheartedly Kwan's love and loyalty, and although she has never identified what she believes the appropriate punishment might be for her emotional frigidity, her guilt is real and it creates a barrier between the two sisters. Finally, although Olivia initiated the quarrel with Simon and asked for the divorce, she is clearly unhappy with their separation. She is afraid to admit the depth of her need for Simon, and to a certain extent her sudden demand for a divorce is an extension of her fear that he might be the one who suggests that they end their marriage. During the life of their relationship, she has managed to convince herself that he does not truly value her presence in his life. Olivia is sure that for Simon she is merely a pallid substitute for Elza, and she is anxious to preempt any move he might make to dissolve the relationship.

Balancing the deaths in the novel and establishing relationships between one life and another is a series of rebirths and reincarnations that produce a sense of cyclical time and universal continuity. The

Changmian-San Francisco connection is integral to the text—essential to both plot and narrative structure. In the scheme of things that Kwan has been articulating since Olivia was a child, Kwan is Nunumu in the nineteenth century story, Olivia is Miss Banner to whom Nunumu pledges her deepest loyalty, and Simon is Yiban, Miss Banner's true love. At the time of her death, Nunumu blames herself for causing the separation of Miss Banner and Yiban, and as Kwan, she is determined to do everything possible to get Olivia and Simon to Changmian where, she tells them, their fate is waiting to happen.

As has been implied, Kwan appears to be at the center of the most mystical rebirths and connections. She tells Olivia that as a child in her second life as Kwan, she drowns with her friend, Buncake. Kwan flies to the World of *Yin*, and there she meets Nelly Banner who is on the verge of returning to life as Olivia. Nelly/Olivia begs Kwan to return to life on earth so that in a few years they can be together again, and Kwan reluctantly obeys, only to discover that her body is so broken that it can no longer support life. With no other alternatives evident, she enters Buncake's unmarred body, and thereafter is her friend's doppelganger, although her mind and heart still belong to the old Kwan. This incident, minor though it appears to be in the almost epic story of Kwan and Olivia, highlights the durability and longevity of the emotional bonds that exist between them, and illustrates the cyclical patterns that inform and undergird the fictional universe of *The Hundred Secret Senses*.

The cycle of death and rebirth is echoed in the legend of Changmian, the village that serves as the setting for Kwan's narratives in two centuries. In Kwan's version of the legend, when the Manchu soldiers ravaged the countryside in the war against the Taiping, Changmian's villagers fled to the nearby caves in the mountains where they concealed themselves. Failing to induce the villagers to come out of their refuges, the soldiers built huge bonfires at the cave entrances, but succeeded only in smoking out thousands of bats whose frantically flapping wings fanned the flames, turning the entire valley, including Changmian, into an inferno. Only two or three soldiers escaped the conflagration, and relief troops who arrived a week later found nothing but a completely, eerily, empty village and hundreds of new graves. But one month later, according to Kwan, a traveler passing Changmian found a thriving village full of people and dogs, all carrying on with their daily activities as though they had been doing so week after week without interruption. To compound the traveler's bafflement and unease, the village people

claimed never to have seen any soldiers. Not surprisingly, once the traveler left the valley and recounted his strange experience, Changmian
acquired a reputation for being a "village of ghosts" (340).

When Olivia and Simon see Changmian for the first time, they notice
immediately that the village appears completely untouched by time.
Changmian's name, which has two possible and opposite meanings, emphasizes the village's timeless and somewhat unearthly appearance, and
foregrounds the contradictions in its history. Kwan tells Olivia and
Simon that the word *chang* means "sing" while *mian* suggests "silk,"
with the combination indicating "something soft but go on forever like
thread" or a never-ending quiet melody (275). She adds, however, that
it is also possible to pronounce Changmian differently, thus producing
a contrasting meaning in which *chang* means "long" and *mian* indicates
"sleep," creating the phrase "long sleep," which is a synonym for death.
Embedded in those two meanings are death and rebirth—the juxtaposition of long sleep with the idea of a soft melody that never ends—the
two constants in Kwan's stories and, it seems, in the relationship between
Kwan and Olivia, and between Olivia and Simon. The rebirth of Changmian, as well as that village's implied participation as the site of Kwan's
own cycle of birth and death and rebirth, makes the village the ideal
place for Olivia's own reconnection with herself. Her story begins in
Changmian and is interrupted there, and she must return not just to the
village but also to the nearby caves to complete and continue the cycle
that is her life.

In *The Secret Language of Dreams*, British psychologist David Fontana
points out that archetypal dreams tend to occur at major transitional
points in life, or during periods of uncertainty and disruption. He adds
further that such dreams "mark the process toward individuation and
spiritual maturity" (34). Olivia is in the midst of an emotionally and
psychologically disruptive transitional point in her life—the break-up of
her marriage to the man whom she has loved more than anyone else in
her entire life. It is no consolation to Olivia to recall that she has precipitated the separation from Simon; her emotional pain is genuine and
devastating. Kwan is likewise at a major transitional point: her fiftieth
birthday, which is a milestone that marks half a century of life. Together,
Olivia and Kwan embark on their shared archetypal quest, the journey
to discover wholeness and integration. Significantly, they travel to a foreign country, an action that in archetypal dreams suggests a journey into
the unconscious in search of wholeness; and their travel to China takes
them to the east, toward a compass point that suggests rebirth and re-

juvenation. They are leaving behind them their San Francisco past, moving toward the landscape of an older shared past, to put their lives in order for the future, which is linked to their shared histories. At the end of the quest, in China, Olivia and Kwan are finally able to rediscover and to assimilate the scattered fragments of their lives and their identities: Kwan is reconciled with Big Ma; Olivia and Simon reconnect; and Olivia acknowledges not just the existence but also the strength and permanence of the bond between herself and Kwan.

Salvation comes to the sisters in different ways. For Kwan, it is the opportunity finally to articulate to Olivia the still-unvoiced remainder of their shared history, to confess the guilt that has burdened her from one lifetime to another because she told the lie that makes her responsible for inadvertently separating Nelly Banner and Yiban Johnson. When she concludes her story on the rainy mountainside near Changmian, she is noticeably relieved. "Now you know all my secret," she tells Olivia. "Give me peace" (343). Her final words are reassurances that Simon loves Olivia, and that Olivia has never been a substitute for Elza. And with that, Kwan enters the secret cave and disappears from Olivia's life. During the week-long search for Kwan, Olivia commences her own journey toward an integrated self as she and Simon slowly begin to re-explore their relationship. Her discovery of the eggs in the Ghost Merchant's garden suggests that new possibilities await her, that her life might change in ways that she has not anticipated.

The novel ends with the final juxtaposition of death and rebirth. Early on the morning of Kwan's disappearance, Simon and Olivia make love for the first time in months on a bed that has belonged to Kwan's family for generations. Nine months later, Olivia gives birth to Samantha, and as Samantha grows into toddlerhood, her favorite toy is the music box that Kwan gave Olivia for a wedding gift. Olivia no longer has Kwan, but in her sister's place is little Samantha whose presence has created a new relationship between her parents. Olivia and Simon have begun to try to resolve their differences, to learn to communicate openly and without rancor, to enjoy being together—with Samantha—as a family. Out of Kwan's death has come life and the strengthening of emotional bonds. And at last, Olivia knows that "the world is not a place but the vastness of the soul. And the soul is nothing more than love, limitless, endless" (358).

Bibliography

WORKS BY AMY TAN

Novels

The Hundred Secret Senses. New York: G.P. Putnam's Sons, 1995.
The Joy Luck Club. New York: G.P. Putnam's Sons, 1989.
The Kitchen God's Wife. New York: G.P. Putnam's Sons, 1991.

Children's Books

The Chinese Siamese Cat. New York: Macmillan Publishing Company, 1994.
The Moon Lady. New York: Macmillan Publishing Company, 1992.

Essays

''The Language of Discretion.'' *The State of the Language*. Eds. Christopher Ricks and Leonard Michaels. Berkeley: University of California Press, 1990.
''Mother Tongue.'' *The Threepenny Review* (Fall 1990).

Short Stories

"Peanut's Fortune." *Grand Street* 10.2 (Winter 1991): 10.
"Two Kinds." *The Atlantic* 263.2 (February 1989): 53.

WORKS ABOUT AMY TAN

Bellafonte, Gina. "People." *Time* 14 September 1992: 79.
Colker, David. "Learn a Little of Her Story." *Los Angeles Times* (22 December 1995): E3.
Giles, Gretchen. "Ghost Writer: Bay Area Author Amy Tan Talks About Fame and Phantoms." *Sonoma Independent.* Http://www.metroactive.com/papers/sonoma/12.14.95.tan-9550.html. 28 February 1997. 5:04 P.M.
Jones, Tod. "Ghost Writer: Amy Tan Explores Themes of Love, Loyalty, and the Hereafter." Http://www.pricecostco.com/pcc/art/ar1295c.html. 28 February 1997. 5:10 P.M.
Kramer, Barbara. *Amy Tan, Author of* The Joy Luck Club. Springfield, NJ: Enslow, 1996.
Lew, Julie. *New York Times* (4 July 1989): 23.
Lipson, Eden Ross. "The Wicked English-Speaking Daughter." *New York Times Book Review* (19 March 1989): 3.
Lyall, Sarah. "A Writer Knows that Spirits Dwell Beyond Her Pages." *New York Times* (29 December 1995): B1.
———. "In the Country of the Spirits: At Home with Writer Amy Tan." *New York Times* (28 December 1995): C1.
Mandell, Jonathan. *New York Newsday* (15 July 1991): Section II, 46.
Merina, Anita. "Joy, Luck, and Literature." *NEA Today* 10.3 (October 1991): 9.
Ross, Val. *Toronto Globe and Mail.* (25 June 1991): 13.
Schleier, Curt. "The Joy Luck Lady." *The Detroit News.* Http://detnews.com/menu/stories/23098.htm. 28 February 1997. 4:40 P.M.
Simpson, Janice C., and Pico Iyer. "Fresh Voices Above the Noisy Din; New Works by Four Chinese-American Writers Splendidly Illustrate the Frustrations, Humor, and Eternal Wonder of the Immigrant's Life." *Time* (3 June 1991): 66.
Somogyi, Barbara, and David Stanton. *Poets and Writers Magazine* 19 (September–October 1991): 24.
"The Spirit Within." *The Salon Interview: Amy Tan.* Http://www.salon1999.com/12nov1995/feature/tan.html. 29 February 1997. 4:53 P.M.
Streitfeld, David. *Washington Post* (8 October 1989): 1.
"Talk by U.S. Writer Amy Tan Prevented." *Los Angeles Times* (1 April 1996): A8.

Tan, Amy. "Amy Tan." *Writers Dreaming*. Ed. Naomi Epel. New York: Carol Southern Books, 1993.

——. "Angst and the Second Novel." *Publisher's Weekly* (5 April 1991): 4.

——. "Lost Lives of Women." *Life* 14.4 (1 April 1991): 90–91.

"Tan, Amy." *Current Biography* 53.2 (February 1992): 55.

Wong, Sau-Ling Cynthia. " 'Sugar Sisterhood': Situating the Amy Tan Phenomenon." *The Ethnic Canon: Histories, Institutions, and Interventions.* Minneapolis: University of Minnesota Press, 1995. 174–210.

Woo, Elaine. *Los Angeles Times* (12 March 1989): Section VI. 1, 14.

Young, Pamela. "Mother with a Past: The Family Album Inspires a Gifted Writer." *MacLean's* (15 July 1991): 47.

REVIEWS AND CRITICISM

The Hundred Secret Senses

Carr, Jo. *Library Journal* (15 May 1996): 100.

Fortuna, Diane. *America* (4 May 1996): 27.

Greenlaw, Lavinia. "The Owl's Story." *Times Literary Supplement* (16 February 1996): 22.

Ives, Nancy R. *Library Journal* (January 1996): 166.

Kakutani, Michiko. "Sisters Looking for Ghosts in China." *New York Times* (17 November 1995): B13

Messud, Claire. "Ghost Story." *New York Times Book Review* (29 October 1995): 11.

Nurse, Donna. "House of the Spirits." *Maclean's* (6 November 1995): 85.

Paik, Felicia. *Ms. Magazine* (November–December 1995): 88.

Pavey, Ruth. "Spirit Levels." *New Statesman & Society* (16 February 1996): 38.

Publisher's Weekly (11 September 1995): 73.

Riley, Sheila. *Library Journal* (15 November 1995): 101.

Scott, Margaret. "California Chinoiserie." *Far Eastern Economic Review* (30 May 1996): 37.

Shapiro, Laura. "Ghost Story." *Newsweek* (6 November 1995): 91.

The Joy Luck Club

Angier, Carole. "*The Joy Luck Club*." *New Statesman and Society* (30 June 1989): 35.

Baker, John F., and Calvin Reid. "Fresh Voices, New Audiences." *Publisher's Weekly* (9 August 1993): 32.

Beard, Carla J. *Amy Tan's The Joy Luck Club*. Piscataway, NJ: Research and Education Assoc., 1996.

Benjamin, Susan J. "*The Joy Luck Club*." *English Journal* 79.6 (October 1990): 82.

Braendlin, Bonnie. "Mother/Daughter Dialog(ic)s In, Around, and About Amy Tan's *The Joy Luck Club*." *Private Voices, Public Lives: Women Speak on the Literary Life*. Ed. Nancy Owen Nelson. Denton: University of North Texas Press, 1995. 111–24.

Davis, Rocio G. "Wisdom (Un) heeded: Chinese Mothers and American Daughters in Amy Tan's *The Joy Luck Club*." *Cuadernos de Investigacion Filologica* 19–20 (1993–94): 89–100.

Donovan, Mary Ann. "*The Joy Luck Club*." *America* (17 November 1990): 372.

Duke, Michael. "Red Ivy, and Green Earth Mother." *World Literature Today* 65.2 (Spring 1991): 361.

Feldman, Gayle. "*The Joy Luck Club*: Chinese Magic, American Blessings, and a Publishing Fairy Tale." *Publisher's Weekly* (7 July 1989): 24.

Fisher, Ann H. "*The Joy Luck Club*." *Library Journal* (15 February 1989): 178.

Fong, Rowena. "*The Joy Luck Club*." *The Gerontologist* 35.2 (April 1995): 284.

Franzen, Jacqueline P. *Breaking Boundaries: The Autobiographical Revolution in Jade Snow Wong's Fifth Chinese Daughter, Maxine Hong Kingston's The Woman Warrior, Amy Tan's The Joy Luck Club, and Edna Wu's Clouds and Rain*. M.A. Thesis. University of Nebraska at Omaha, 1996.

Gates, David. "*The Joy Luck Club*." *Newsweek* (17 April 1989): 68–69.

Gavioli, Davida. "In Search of the Mother's Lost Voice: Mariama Bâ's *Une si longue lettre*, Francesca Sanvitale's *Madre e figlia*, and Amy Tan's *The Joy Luck Club*." *DAI* 55.6 (December 1994): DAI Number 9428101.

Heung, Marina. "Daughter-text/Mother-text: Matrilineage in Amy Tan's *Joy Luck Club*." *Feminist Studies* 19 (Fall 1993): 597.

Ho, Khanh. "*The Kitchen God's Wife*." *Amerasia Journal* 19.2 (Spring 1993): 181.

Ho, Wendy Ann. "Mother and Daughter Writing and the Politics of Location in Maxine Hong Kingston's *The Woman Warrior* and Amy Tan's *The Joy Luck Club*." *DAI* 54.7 (January 1994): DAI Number 9320902.

———. "Swan-Feather Mothers and Coca-Cola Daughters: Teach Tan's *The Joy Luck Club*." *Teaching American Ethnic Literatures: Nineteen Essays*. Ed. John R. Maitino and David R. Peck. Albuquerque: University of New Mexico Press, 1996. 327–45.

Hoffman, Preston. "Book Sounds." *Wilson Library Bulletin* 69. 7 (March 1995): 99.

Koenig, Rhoda. "*The Joy Luck Club*." *New York* 22.12 (20 March 1989): 82.

Miner, Valerie. "*The Joy Luck Club*." *Nation* (24 April 1989): 566.

Nathan, Paul. "Tan Teams up for Encore." *Publisher's Weekly* (5 September 1994): 20.

Ong, Caroline. "Roots Relations." *Times Literary Supplement* (29 December 1989): 1447.

Pollard, D. E. "Much Ado About Identity." *Far Eastern Economic Review* (27 July 1989): 41.

Schell, Orville. "*The Joy Luck Club*." *New York Times Book Review* (19 March 1989): 3.

Schueller, Malini Johar. "Theorizing Ethnicity and Subjectivity: Maxine Hong Kingston's *Tripmaster Monkey* and Amy Tan's *The Joy Luck Club*." *Genders* 15 (Winter 1992): 72.

Shear, Walter. "Generation Differences and the Diaspora in *The Joy Luck Club*." *Critique: Studies in Contemporary Fiction* 34.3 (Spring 1993): 193–99.

Shen, Gloria. "Born of a Stranger: Mother-Daughter Relationships and Storytelling in Amy Tan's *The Joy Luck Club*." *International Women's Writing: New Landscapes of Identity*. Ed. Anne E. Brown and Marjanne E. Gooze. Westport, CT: Greenwood Press, 1995. 233–44.

Skow, John. "Tiger Ladies." *Time* (27 March 1989): 98.

Smith, Jayne R. *The Joy Luck Club: A Curriculum Unit*. Rocky River, OH: Center for Learning, 1994.

Souris, Stephen. " 'Only Two Kinds of Daughters': Inter-monologue Dialogicity in *The Joy Luck Club*." *MELUS* 19.2 (Summer 1994): 99–123.

Spalding, Frances. "*The Joy Luck Club*." *Times Educational Supplement* (4 August 1989): 19.

Steinberg, Sybil, and Genevieve Stuttaford. "*The Joy Luck Club*." *Publisher's Weekly* (23 December 1988): 66.

Sterritt, David. "*The Joy Luck Club*." *Christian Science Monitor* (16 September 1993): 11.

Sweeting, Paul, and John Zinsser. "*The Joy Luck Club*." *Publisher's Weekly* (7 July 1989): 37.

Tynan, Laurie. "*The Joy Luck Club*." *Library Journal* (July 1989): 123.

Wang, Dorothy. "*The Joy Luck Club*." *Newsweek* (17 April 1989): 69.

Xu, Ben. "Memory and the Ethnic Self: Reading Amy Tan's *The Joy Luck Club*." *Memory, Narrative, and Identity: New Essays in Ethnic American Literatures*. Ed. Amritjit Singh, Joseph T. Skerrett, Jr., and Robert E. Hogan. Boston: Northeastern University Press, 1994.

Movie and Theater Reviews

Book, Esther Wachs. "*Joy Luck Club* Plays in China: Theatrical Version to be Staged in Five Cities." *Far Eastern Economic Review* (26 August 1993): 31.

Buck, Joan Juliet. *Vogue* (October 1993): 215.

Denby, David. "*The Joy Luck Club*." *New York* (20 September 1993): 64.

Johnson, Brian. *Maclean's* (27 September 1993): 70.

Klawans, Stuart. *The Nation* (4 October 1993): 364.

Maslin, Janet. "*The Joy Luck Club*." *New York Times* (8 September 1993): C15.

———. "*The Joy Luck Club.*" *New York Times* (25 March 1994): D17.
———. "Intimate Lessons of Family and Culture Available to All." *Migration World Magazine* 22.1 (January–February 1994): 37.
McCarthy, Todd. "*The Joy Luck Club.*" *Variety* (13 September 1993): 32.
McGinnis, John. "*The Joy Luck Club.*" *Wall Street Journal* (19 August 1993): A8.
Salomon, Julie. "*The Joy Luck Club.*" *Wall Street Journal* (9 September 1993): A18.
Shapiro, Laura. "The Generation Gap in Chinatown." *Newsweek* (27 September 1993): 70.
Simon, John. "Chinoiserie." *National Review* (15 November 1993): 61.
Tyler, Patrick. "*The Joy Luck Club.*" *New York Times* (27 November 1993): N9.

The Kitchen God's Wife

Caesar, Judith. "Patriarchy, Imperialism, and Knowledge in *The Kitchen God's Wife.*" *North Dakota Quarterly* 62.4 (Fall 1994): 164–74.
Dew, Rob Forman. "*The Kitchen God's Wife.*" *New York Times Book Review* (16 June 1991): 9.
Fisher, Ann. H. "*The Kitchen God's Wife.*" *Library Journal* (1 June 1991): 198.
Ho, Khanh. *Amerasia Journal* 19.2 (Spring 1993): 181.
Hughes, Kathryn. "*The Kitchen God's Wife.*" *New Stateman and Society* (12 July 1991): 37.
Hunt, Adam Paul. "*The Kitchen God's Wife.*" *Library Journal* (July 1991): 154.
Iyer, Pico. "The Second Triumph of Amy Tan." *Time* (3 June 1991): 67.
Koenig, Rhoda. "Nanking Pluck." *New York* (17 June 1991): 83.
Maryles, Daisy. "Behind the Bestsellers." *Publisher's Weekly* (18 May 1992): 27.
New, W. H. "*The Kitchen God's Wife.*" *Canadian Literature* 133 (Summer 1992): 194.
Ong, Caroline. "Re-Writing the Old Wives Tales." *Times Literary Supplement* (5 July 1991): 20.
Schwartz, Eleanor N. "The Kitchen God's Wife." *Far Eastern Economic Review* (14 November 1991): 56.
Schwartz, Gil. "*The Kitchen God's Wife.*" *Fortune* (26 August 1991): 116.
Shapiro, Laura. "*The Kitchen God's Wife.*" *Newsweek* (24 June 1991): 63.
Steinberg, Sybil. "*The Kitchen God's Wife.*" *Publisher's Weekly* (12 April 1991): 45.
Zia, Helen. "*The Kitchen God's Wife.*" *Ms.* (November–December 1991): 76.

Other Fictional Works by Amy Tan

Publisher's Weekly. Vol. 239.32–33 (20 July 1992): 249. (*The Moon Lady*)
Publisher's Weekly. Vol. 239.50 (16 November 1992): 24. (*The Moon Lady*)
Publisher's Weekly. Vol. 241.28 (11 July 1994): 78. (*The Chinese Siamese Cat*)

Riordan, James. *Times Educational Supplement* (5 February 1993): R10. (*The Moon Lady*)

Roback, Diane, and Shannon Maughan. "Fall 1992 Children's Books." *Publisher's Weekly* (20 July 1992): 35.

Schecter, Ellen. "*The Moon Lady*." *New York Times Book Review* (8 November 1992): 31.

Additional Resources on Amy Tan's Novels

McCart Drolet, Anne. *Telling Her Stories to Change the Con(text) of Identity: Four Novels by Contemporary American Women Authors of Color. DAI* 54.8 (February 1994): DAI Number 9402954.

Mitchell, David Thomas. *Conjured Communities: The Multiperspectival Novels of Amy Tan, Toni Morrison, Julia Alvares, Louise Erdrich, and Christina Garcia. DAI* 54.11 (May 1994): DAI Number 9409768.

Peter, Nelson, and Peter Freundlich. "Women We Love: Nine Who Knock Us Out." *Esquire* (August 1989): 86.

Reid, E. Shelley. *The Compound I: Narrative and Identity in the Novels of Toni Morrison, Louise Erdrich, and Amy Tan. DAI* 55.11 (May 1995): DAI Number 9509148.

Ryan, Marya Mae. *Gender and Community: Womanist and Feminist Perspectives in the Fiction of Toni Morrison, Amy Tan, Sandra Cisneros, and Louise Erdrich. DAI* 56.9 (March 1996): DAI Number 9543711.

Smorada, Claudia Kovach. "Side-Stepping Death: Ethnic Identity, Contradiction, and the Mother(land) in Amy Tan's Novels." *Fu Jen Studies: Literature & Linguistics* 24 (1991): 31–45.

SECONDARY SOURCES

Asian Women United of California, eds. *Making Waves: An Anthology of Writings by and about Asian American Women*. Boston: Beacon, 1989.

Bibliographic Index. New York: Wilson, 1937–. Monthly.

Chen, Victoria. "Chinese American Women, Language, and Moving Subjectivity." *Women and Language* 18.1 (Spring 1995): 3–7.

Cheung, King-Kok. *Asian-American Literature: An Annotated Bibliography*. New York: MLA, 1988.

Chiu, Christina. *Notable Asian Americans: Literature and Education*. New York: Chelsea House, 1995.

Chua, Cheng Lok. "Two Chinese Versions of the American Dream: The Golden Mountain in Lin Yutang and Maxine Hong Kingston." *MELUS* 8.4 (Winter 1981): 61–70.

Donnerstag, Jurgen. "Literary Reading and Intercultural Learning—Understand-
    ing Ethnic American Fiction in the EFL Classroom." *Amerikastudien* 37
    (1992): 595–611.

Downing, Christine. *Psyche's Sisters: Re-Imagining the Meaning of Sisterhood*. San
    Francisco: Harper and Row, 1988.

Duke, Michael S., ed. *Modern Chinese Women Writers: Critical Appraisals*. New
    York: M. E. Sharpe, 1989.

Editors of Time-Life Books. *China*. Amsterdam: Time-Life Books, 1984.

Feldman, Gayle. "Spring's Five Fictional Encounters of the Chinese American
    Kind." *Publisher's Weekly* (8 February 1991): 25.

Goldman, Marlene. "Naming the Unspeakable: The Mapping of Female Identity
    in Maxine Hong Kingston's *The Woman Warrior*." *International Women's
    Writing: New Landscapes of Identity*. Eds. Anne E. Brown and Marjanne E.
    Goozé. Westport, CT: Greenwood Press, 1995. 223–32.

Hawley, John C. "Assimilation and Resistance in Female Fiction of Immigration:
    Bharati Mukherjee, Amy Tan, and Christine Bell." *Rediscovering America
    1492–1992: National, Cultural, and Disciplinary Boundaries Re-Examined*. Eds.
    Leslie Barry, Janet Gold, Marketta Laurila, Arnulfo Ramirez, Joseph Ri-
    capito, and Jesus Torrecilla. Baton Rouge: Louisiana State University Press,
    1992. 226–34.

Hongo, Garrett, ed. *Under Western Eyes: Personal Essays From Asian America*. New
    York: Anchor Books/ Doubleday, 1995.

Hsaio, Ruth. "Facing the Incurable: Patriarchy in *Eat a Bowl of Tea*." *Reading the
    Literature of Asian America*. Eds. Shirley Geok-lin Lim and Amy Ling. Phil-
    adelphia: Temple University Press, 1992. 151–62.

Kim, Elaine. *Asian American Literature: An Introduction to the Writings and their
    Social Context*. Philadelphia: Temple University Press, 1982.

Kim, Elaine, et al. *Making More Waves: New Writing by Asian American Women*.
    Boston: Beacon Press, 1997.

Kim, Hying-chan. *Asian-American Studies: An Annotated Bibliography and Research
    Guide*. New York: Greenwood Press, 1986.

Lim, Shirley Geok-Lin. "Feminist and Ethnic Literary Theories in Asian American
    Literature." *Feminist Studies* 19.3 (Fall 1993): 571–95.

Lim, Shirley G., and Amy Ling. *Reading the Literatures of Asian America*. Phila-
    delphia: Temple University Press, 1992.

Ling, Amy. *Between Worlds: Women Writers of Chinese Ancestry*. New York: Per-
    gamon, 1990.

Marvis, Barbara J. *Contemporary American Success Stories: Famous People of Asian
    Ancestry* Vol 4. Childs, MD: Mitchell Lane, 1995.

Noda, Kesaya E. "Growing Up Asian in America." *Making Waves: An Anthology
    of Writings By and About Asian American Women*. Ed. Asian Women United
    of California. Boston: Beacon, 1989. 244.

Palumbo-Liu, David, ed. *The Ethnic Canon: Histories, Institutions, and Interventions.* Minneapolis: University of Minnesota Press, 1995.

Pearlman, Mickey and Katherine Usher Henderson. *Inter/View: Talks with America's Writing Women.* Lexington: University Press of Kentucky, 1990.

Peck, David R. *American Ethnic Literatures: Native American, African & American, Chicano/Latino, and Asian American Writers and Their Backgrounds: An Annotated Bibliography.* Pasadena, CA: Salem Press, 1992.

Rabinowitz, Paula. "Eccentric Memories: A Conversation with Maxine Hong Kingston." *Michigan Quarterly Review* 26 (Winter 1987): 177–87.

Ruoff, A. LaVonne, and Jerry W. Ward, Jr. *Redefining American Literary History.* New York: MLA, 1990.

Singh, Amritjit, Joseph T. Skerrett, Jr., and Robert E. Hogan. *Memory, Narrative, and Identity: New Essays in Ethnic American Literatures.* Boston: Northeastern University Press, 1994.

Takaki, Ronald. *Strangers From a Different Shore: A History of Asian Americans.* Boston: Little, Brown, 1989.

Taylor, Chris, et al. *China: A Lonely Planet Travel Survival Kit.* 3rd ed. Hawthorn, Australia: Lonely Planet Publications, 1993.

Wang, Veronica. "The Chinese-American Woman's Quest for Identity." *MELUS* 12.3 (1985): 23–31.

Wei, William. *The Asian American Movement.* Philadelphia: Temple University Press, 1993.

Wong, Sau-ling C. *Reading Asian American Literature: From Necessity to Extravagance.* Princeton, NJ: Princeton University Press, 1993.

Index

About the Author

E. D. HUNTLEY is author of *V. C. Andrews: A Critical Companion* (Greenwood Press, 1996). She is Professor of English and Associate Dean of Graduate Studies at Appalachian State University in Boone, North Carolina. In addition to her administrative duties, she teaches courses in drama. She is preparing a two-volume anthology of Native American plays and *First Nations: A Research Guide to Native American Drama*; she has also begun work on a book about Maxine Hong Kingston's works.